INTRODUCING

Camus

David Zane Mairowitz and Alain Korkos

Edited by Richard Appignanesi

ICON BOOKS UK   TOTEM BOOKS USA

This edition published in the UK
in 1999 by Icon Books Ltd.,
Grange Road, Duxford,
Cambridge CB2 4QF
email: icon@mistral.co.uk
www.iconbooks.co.uk

Distributed in the UK, Europe,
Canada, South Africa and Asia by the
Penguin Group: Penguin Books Ltd.,
27 Wrights Lane, London W8 5TZ

This edition published in Australia
in 1999 by Allen & Unwin Pty. Ltd.,
PO Box 8500, 9 Atchison Street,
St. Leonards NSW 2065

Previously published in the UK and
Australia in 1998 under the title
Camus for Beginners

First published in the United States
in 1998 by Totem Books
Inquiries to: PO Box 223,
Canal Street Station,
New York, NY 10013

In the United States,
distributed to the trade by
National Book Network Inc.,
4720 Boston Way, Lanham,
Maryland 20706

Library of Congress Catalog
Card Number: 97–062431

Text copyright © 1998 David Zane Mairowitz
Illustrations copyright © 1998 Alain Korkos

The author and artist have asserted their moral rights.

Originating editor: Richard Appignanesi

Printed and bound in Australia
by McPherson's Printing Group, Victoria

4 January 1960. Afternoon. Outside the French town of Petit-Villeblevin near Montereau on the RN5, 24 kilometres from the town of Sens, just south of Paris, a Facel-Véga swerves off the road into a tree, smashing the automobile to smithereens. Inside, in the passenger seat, killed on impact, the Nobel Prize-winning author, Albert Camus.

According to the dashboard clock, time stops for him at 13.55.
In the wreckage, amongst his papers, the partly revised, handwritten, highly illegible manuscript of an unfinished novel …

LE PREMIER HOMME
(THE FIRST MAN)

IN PARIS THERE WAS A GREAT DEAL OF UNEMPLOYMENT AND UNREST AND THE CONSTITUENT ASSEMBLY VOTED FIFTY MILLION FRANCS TO SEND OFF A COLONY OF SETTLERS...

A chapter in the novel flashes back 112 years to just after the Revolution of 1848. The French government, like its English counterpart, sends its problem population (mostly unemployed, but also revolutionaries and criminals) overseas to its newly-conquered territories. The French invasion and conquest of Algeria had begun in 1830, but much of the huge land mass remained uncolonized. Now the new settlers are promised a home as well as 2-10 hectares of land each. Over a thousand families volunteer to make the journey.

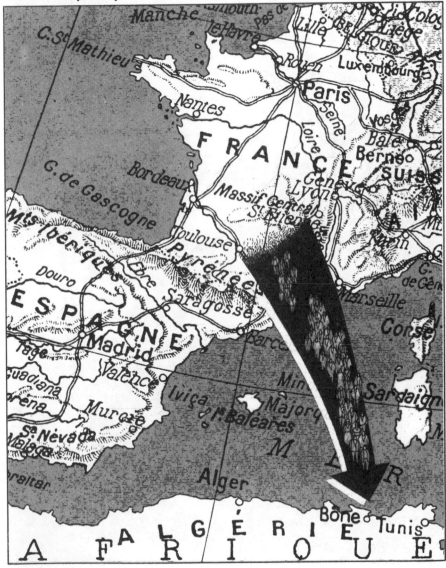

SIX BARGES DRAWN BY CART HORSES, WITH THE CITY'S BRASS BAND PLAYING *LA MARSEILLAISE* AND *LE CHANT DU DÉPART*, THE PRIESTS BLESSING THEM ON THE BANKS OF THE SEINE, WITH A FLAG BEARING THE NAME OF AN AS YET NON-EXISTENT VILLAGE, WHICH THE PASSENGERS WOULD CREATE THEMSELVES THROUGH MAGIC.

For the voyage across the Mediterranean, the passengers change to a paddle-boat, ironically called – given their hot destination – *The Labrador*.

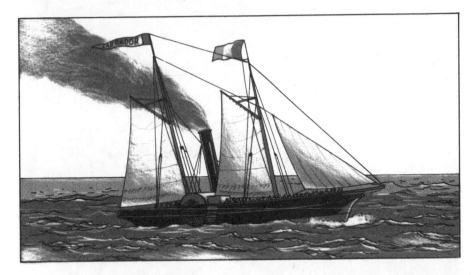

At the first sighting of the Algerian coast …

THOSE DARK MASSES, THOSE SHARP, DISLOCATED PIECES OF NIGHT, THAT WAS KABYLIA, THE WILD AND BLOODY PART OF THIS COUNTRY...

The ancestors of Albert Camus were probably not amongst these pioneer settlers (they would come slightly later) arriving at the port of Bône (the town where St Augustine had lived). Yet this key scene out of his "autobiographical" novel will pave the way for an understanding of his lifelong obsession with his native Algeria, one which will leave him isolated in the wake of a major political disagreement with the French intellectual establishment and which can explain equally the despair as well as the punishing **sunlight** of his major works.

These first "*pied-noir*"* families are Camus' very own salt-of-the-earth, working-class settlers (whom he will always insist are **not colonizers**). His own family will inherit the hardships of these pioneers of 1848, along with the silent enmity of the native Arab population …

THERE WAS NO ROAD FOR THE IMMIGRANTS: THE WOMEN AND CHILDREN CROWDED ONTO THE ARMY'S ARTILLERY CARRIAGES, THE MEN ON FOOT, CUTTING BY INSTINCT THROUGH THE SWAMPY PLAIN AND THICKET, UNDER THE HOSTILE GAZE OF ODD GROUPS OF ARABS WATCHING THEM FROM A DISTANCE...

*The expression "*pied-noir*" is first associated, just before World War I, with those Algerian infantrymen who wore white gaiters over black shoes. The expression disappears during the 1930s, only to return in France in 1955 when it is used to describe the European Algerian population, most of whom leave Algeria during the war for independence.

Followed by malaria, cholera, sunstroke and murderous attacks by the local population, until "*two-thirds of the immigrants died … without ever having touched a spade or plough.*"

Le Premier Homme is not strictly autobiographical, but it demonstrates the way in which an author like Camus is able to fictionalize real obsessions and give them an order which is often more "real" than autobiography. Thus he **dramatizes** his own birth on 7 November 1913.

On the road to a small village outside Bône in Algeria, near the Tunisian border, a carriage braves the difficult roads before a rainstorm.

TO THE LEFT OF THE ROAD AND A LITTLE FURTHER, THEY COULD MAKE OUT THE LIGHTS OF SOLFERINO OBSCURED BY THE RAIN.

Inside the farmhouse, the two men set up a mattress by the fireplace.

After a time …

This scene, written towards the end of his life, is a rare moment in Camus' fiction, showing a hint of natural fraternity between a Moslem Arab and a *pied-noir*. An untiring champion of Arab rights in Algeria, Camus was scarcely able to translate these efforts into personal relationships.

The man standing under the sack in the rain, called "Henri Cormery" in the novel, is the "first man", Lucien Camus (1885-1914), the first male figure in the life of his son, Albert. That he will be killed a year later at the Battle of the Marne means that the boy will never really know his father, a fact which will oblige him to create a personal myth around this figure and transform him into fiction. Until he finds his father's grave later in life, when he is a man already older than the one killed in World War I, two images stand out above all for the son Albert (or "Jacques" in the novel).

The French military authorities were considerate enough to send the widow Camus the piece of German shrapnel found in her husband's body, a memento she would keep forever after in a biscuit tin.

The second and more lasting image is one which Camus will use again and again in his fiction and which forms the basis of his lifelong passionate battle against all forms of capital punishment. His clearest evocation of this story can be found in his *Réflexions sur la guillotine* (*Reflections on the Guillotine*, 1957). Before World War I, an agricultural worker had massacred a family of farmers and their children and was condemned to death by decapitation, which Camus' father, a staunch believer in the guillotine, considered too "lenient" a punishment.

ONE OF THE RARE THINGS I KNOW ABOUT HIM IS THAT, FOR THE FIRST TIME IN HIS LIFE, HE WANTED TO WITNESS AN EXECUTION.
HE NEVER TOLD ANYONE WHAT HE SAW THAT MORNING. MY MOTHER TELLS ONLY THAT HE RUSHED INTO THE HOUSE, REFUSING TO SPEAK... AND QUITE SUDDENLY BEGAN TO VOMIT.

In fact, concludes Camus, his father could no longer think of the murdered children, but only of the condemned man's body tossed onto the guillotine block in order to be beheaded.

If his father remains out of focus, and only elaborated in his last book, there is hardly a more vivid picture in Camus' life than that of his mother. Catherine Sintès Camus, of Spanish descent, who worked as a "*femme de ménage*" (charwoman), was illiterate and partially deaf, and completely dominated by her own mother, to whose household she meekly returned after her husband's death. If there is any real tenderness to be found in the works of Albert Camus (a microscope's task), it is in regard to the image of this woman, sitting idly by her Algiers window, indifferently watching life pass her by.

At the same time, the young Camus is aware that this object of affection is somehow lost to him. Coming in upon her seated alone at dusk …

...HER EYES VAGUE, LOST IN FOLLOWING THE LINE OF A CRACK IN THE PARQUET FLOOR.
NIGHT DARKENS ALL AROUND HER, THE SILENCE BECOMING HOPELESS DESOLATION...

"He pities his mother, but is it the same as loving her? She has never caressed him because she wouldn't know how … And feeling thus detached from her, he can begin to understand her unhappiness."
Entre Oui et Non (*Between Yes and No*, 1935).

Albert Camus' mother remained virtually all her life in Algiers, and the equation **Maman=Algérie=Maman** is one the author will never be able to escape. Even his later controversial positions on the Algerian uprising are coloured by her presence on the scene.

Almost nothing he ever wrote or said about Algeria can thus be seen from an objective standpoint. Spending nearly all his adult life in French exile, Algeria remains nonetheless his major reference point. And all of his important works of fiction are set on Algerian soil.

At the time of Camus' birth, Algeria was officially considered as consisting of three French "*départements*" and a colony. In 1913, France's position in the country was elaborated by the governor-general: to substitute "*civilization and common sense for barbarism and fanaticism, which means the assimilation, unification and Frenchifying of the races.*"

France is the mother country with her kings and *châteaux*, and young Moslems as well as *pieds-noirs* are imbued at school with the idea of a **common heritage** between the two countries, learning – cynically – about "**our** ancestors the Gauls", while being taught virtually nothing of the thirteen centuries of Algerian history between the Roman and French colonizations.

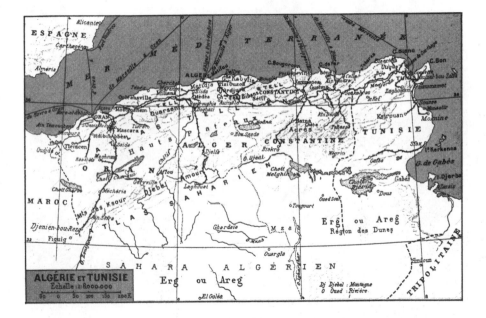

MAP OF ALGERIA AND TUNISIA IN 1913

The idea that Algeria was **an integral part of France** will always set the Algerian question apart from most other colonial experiences, even those of France in Indo-China or indeed in Morocco and Tunisia. When, 130 years later, French Algerians are forced to leave, they will not see themselves as victims of de-colonialization, but as having been kicked out of **their own country**.

Like any number of *pieds-noirs*, the child Albert Camus grows up with this double identity. At once a denizen of the North African landscape, he will always be a product of French culture and language. He could speak neither Arabic nor Berber, the two major native languages of the country.

His own childhood being one of working-class poverty (although not to be compared in misery with that of the Arab population), he always makes the distinction between hard-core colonialists and ordinary *pieds-noirs*. He believes the two communities can live together and, up to the end of his life, he would never be able to accept the idea of an independent Algeria.

The Belcourt district of Algiers where Camus grew up lay on the peripheries of the Marabout Arab quarter behind which was one of the largest slum areas of the city. It was a neighbourhood of low-paid French Algerians, craftsmen or factory workers, like Camus' Uncle Etienne who worked as a cooper in a barrel-making *atelier*, which is evoked years later by the author in the short-story …

Les Muets

(The Silent Ones)

In this story, from the 1957 collection **L'Exil et le royaume** (**Exile and the Kingdom**), a failed strike brings a bitter and tense atmosphere to the workshop between workers and the boss …

… until the latter's small child is taken off to hospital in an emergency, and the natural humanity of the situation (as always in Camus) overrides the strongest political positions.

WHILE UNDRESSING IN HER ROOM, THE CHILD SUDDENLY FELL OVER AS IF SHE'D BEEN CUT DOWN.

INCREDIBLE !

But what makes "*Les Muets*" important for a retrospective understanding of the young Albert Camus is the symbolic **community** in the cooperage, with its French Algerians, an Arab worker, Saïd, and even one named Esposito, to represent the large Spanish *pied-noir* contingent. This image of the poor, honest, **mixed** Algeria is one the author will always cherish nostalgically and later fight for politically, even with all the historical odds against him.

Unlike most of his contemporaries on the French literary scene (many of whom were products of the famous Parisian *grandes écoles)*, Camus' background was decidedly anti-intellectual. There was not a book or magazine to be found in his household, and Grandmother Sintès ruled with an iron fist, insisting that Camus and his brother do an obligatory minimum of schooling and then go out to work. It was probably only at the insistence of one of his primary school teachers, Louis Germain, that Albert Camus the writer was plucked from the jaws of obscurity.

At the same time, there was **soccer**. Later in life, and in his novel **La Chute** (**The Fall**, 1956) Camus would declare that the only places on earth where he felt really happy and relaxed were in a theatre building or in a football stadium. Young Albert played in goal for *Racing Universitaire d'Alger* from 1928-30, and there is no doubt this would remain a great passion throughout his life. He would also later claim that his entire sense of ethics was learned on the soccer pitch.

Yet an event in 1930 would condemn him to remain thereafter a spectator rather than a player. Camus began coughing up blood and the first signs of **tuberculosis** were diagnosed, an illness which his body would carry as a personal plague all his life.

There is no doubt that this fact plays a central role in the insistence on **death and mortality** in most of his work. Aside from other multiple interpretations, his novel *La Peste* (*The Plague*, 1947) can also be read as a private baptism of fire, a metaphoric journey through his own pulmonary system.

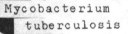

Mycobacterium tuberculosis

That his body betrayed him on the cusp of his young manhood has a particular irony here, and one which is key to the development of his personality. For a French Algerian, the symbolic pulse of life is no doubt the **Mediterranean** which links the two sides of his identity.

Camus was then – and would always remain – a Mediterranean man. As a healthy youth, this would take the form of the traditional paganism which he believed had been handed down from the ancient Greeks with their cult of beauty and the body. In its most "banal" aspect, young Albert Camus was a devotee of sun, sand, swimming, and was by no means immune to the pressures of classic machismo which come with the territory.

In his first book of essays **L'Envers et l'Endroit**, 1935 (known in English, for better or worse, as **Betwixt and Between**), he would claim, after having glimpsed the "cold suburbs" of Europe, that even the poorest Mediterranean Arab was less miserable because he had the sun and a sky that was clear over his head. As for himself, he said later, in describing his Algerian youth: "*In order to make up for a natural indifference, I was placed midway between misery and the sun. Misery stopped me from believing that all is well under the sun and in history; the sun taught me that history isn't everything.*"

Later, Camus would try to promote a real Mediterranean culture, one which could unite its two coasts in a common identity. This was far removed from the "Latinity" which Fascist propaganda would soon claim for the same sea basin, an over-blown sense of pride and historical domination inherited from the Romans. For Camus, the model was chiefly the Greek one which, he believed, creates men of **balance** (*mesure*) who above all **know their own limits**.

In any case, he would almost never get the punishing Mediterranean sun out of his eyes, even in his darkest European hours. One of the models of the "absurd" man is the Spanish Don Juan, and there is no doubt that the godless "**indifference of the universe**", which forms the heart of his relation to religion and life, is the vision of a man born to peel back that ever-blue Mediterranean sky and see the glaring truth that there is **nothing but Nothing** behind it.

Nowhere is Camus more lyrical about the Mediterranean world than in his book of essays **Noces** (**Nuptials**, 1938), where he displays a nearly-pagan worship of nature, bedazzled by this particular Algerian landscape linking two vastnesses, the sea and the Sahara. Visiting the Roman ruins at **Tipasa** on Algeria's western coast, he writes a hymn to the naked and purely sensual pleasures of this world. But it is here also that Camus' vision of **the Absurd** has its first stirrings. The sky and sea and silence manifest "*lucidity, indifference, the true signs of despair and of beauty*".

In the essay "*Le vent à Djemila*" ("The Wind at Djemila"), he reminds his reader of the influence of the Greeks and Romans who "*face their destiny ... by embracing death.*" As for himself, "***it doesn't please me to believe that death leads to another life***. *For me it is a closed door. I'm not saying it is not a step that has to be taken: but it is **a horrible and dirty adventure**.*" An "adventure" made more palatable facing the sea and the dazzling sky, for in this landscape death is not divorced from everyday reality, not mystified as in other (e.g. European) cultures. It is merely closure to a series of gestures in the face of overwhelming (but "tender") **indifference**

When the left-wing alliance, *Le Front Populaire*, came to power in France in 1936 under the premiership of **Léon Blum** (1872-1950), Camus, like many French intellectuals of the time, saw in it the best means of defeating the Fascist tendencies which were rising in France as well as across the Pyrénées in Spain. The crushing of the Spanish Republic would always remain a key experience for Camus, and his fierce opposition to Franco would continue right up until his death, even after such opposition ceased to be fashionable.

But the innate injustice of the Algerian situation was the real breeding ground for his political education. Even when Camus was convinced in 1934 to join the Communist Party (CP) with its international bent, his concern and emphasis would always be Algeria, however much he grieved for the state of the world-at-large.

Unlike many of his contemporaries, Camus had few illusions about the CP and was never a convert to Marxist-Leninism. For him, the Party was chiefly a means of righting the inequality on his home territory, and the "Arab Question" was his main brief as a Communist Party worker in his own Belcourt *quartier*. The indigenous Moslem population had been denied the basic civil rights which French Algerians had. In 1934, the Party line was to gather Algerian, Moroccan and Tunisian Communists and create an organization independent of the French CP. One of Camus' jobs was recruiting new members from the Arab proletariat. In 1936, the Algerian Communist Party (PCA) was founded in Algiers, with the ultimate aim – although it was never that of Albert Camus – of autonomy from France.

Yet it was not very long before the axe of Stalinist "*realpolitik*" fell, bringing Camus' Communist adventure to an abrupt close. The stance of the Algerian branch of the CP had been, naturally, anti-colonialist and thus a danger to the security of France. All of which worked out quite well for the Comintern until the Stalin-Laval Pact of 1935, in which the former recognized the necessity for France to remain strong in the face of Hitler. This meant keeping a tight lid on the French CP, especially in Algeria, where now the fight against Fascism would have to **precede** that against colonialism, because anything that could weaken France would ultimately strengthen the Nazis and thereby endanger the USSR. This effectively eliminated Camus' main reason for adhering to the Party in the first place.

It would get worse. Camus was seen to frequent a breakaway group, *Le Parti du Peuple Algérien*, who were labelled (typically) as Fascists by the Stalinoid CP. In classic fashion, Camus was damned as a Trotskyist, "put on trial" and expelled from the Party.

That this experience contributed to his anti-Communist bias after World War II and throughout the 1950s is probable, but it did not deter the young Camus from pursuing his efforts to call attention to the plight of Moslems in Algeria. Soon he would wear a cap that he would never lose – that of **"moral journalist"** – one which would also affect his fictional style. Like many before and after him, he was discovering that undefined territory between literature and engaged journalism.

In 1938, he became a reporter for the newly-founded *Alger Républicain*, a left-wing daily which would attempt to adapt Popular Front ideology to local conditions. Camus was responsible for covering Algiers, which included local political and social matters as well as the criminal courts, and this latter brief would serve him well later when writing ***L'Étranger*** (***The Stranger***, 1942). Above all, he singled out injustices, whether social or judicial, wrote *exposés* where he smelled scandal, and generally supported the underdogs and victims of society's *misère* (a word which appears over and over in his journalistic work). He also wrote most of his articles in the **first person**, up until then a rarity in French reporting.

Camus' **subjective** concern can be felt in his articles. In the trial of ten agricultural workers arrested for arson, he wrote that sending such men to prison was "*a personal injury for each of us*".

This is even more evident in his famous series of eleven articles from 1939, **Misère de la Kabylie**. Kabylia, a group of *massifs* in the north-eastern part of Algeria, populated essentially by Berbers, was amongst the most poverty-stricken regions of the country. Camus was genuinely shocked by the misery he found there and his articles are extraordinary for their use of a deft blend of reportage – he knows how many sacks of wheat are consumed per year and how much each worker is paid in each region – with a strong editorial bent.

The writing is "objective" in the best classical journalistic tradition, but the writer leaves no doubt about his sympathies.
"*One morning, in Tizi-Ouzou, I saw children in rags fighting Kabyle dogs for the contents of a dustbin.*" Or "*It is contemptible to say these people don't have the same needs as we do.*" Or "*Working conditions in Kabylia are those of slavery.*" The son of poor *pieds-noirs* is sickened by the sight of a much deeper poverty: schoolchildren fainting from hunger, villages without doctors or sanitation.

Although he talks about "*the general contempt in which the colonialist holds the unhappy people of this country*", Camus already shows himself to be against independence for Algeria. Instead, "*we have to knock down the walls which separate*" French Algerians from the native population, because "*a regime which separates Algeria from France does harm to our country*". Going even further, he postulates the sort of naive notion which some years later will earn him derision from the Left:

"*If colonial conquest can ever find an excuse, it is in the sense of helping the conquered people to keep its personality.*" What makes Camus' journalism special, however, is its literary nature. Describing a twilight climb up a mountain where he could see the Berber fires below in the valley: "*I knew … it would have been lovely to be swept up in such a … marvellous evening, but that the misery seen in the blazing fires opposite seemed to ban all the beauty of the world.*"

By late 1938, the Right was effectively back in power in France, and Algeria – with its extreme right-wing tendencies – was a reflection of the mainland. With war approaching, the non-violent Albert Camus tried to enlist, but was turned down because of his tuberculosis. There was nothing for him to do but continue his career as a journalist, becoming editor-in-chief of the two-page *Soir Républicain* after *Alger Républicain* was forced to shut down.

But the new paper quickly ran afoul of the draconian military censorship in Algeria. Decidedly pacifist in its editorial content, *Soir Républicain* fostered the idea that war was **not** inevitable and saw itself as a moral opposition to the forces of impending world catastrophe. A typical (unsigned but certainly Camusian) editorial: "*Mankind's only greatness is to struggle against that which overwhelms it. It isn't happiness we should seek today, but much more than that, a kind of greatness-in-despair.*"

For these kinds of sentiments, the newspaper was closed down by the censor in January 1940. Now a "threat to national security", Albert Camus is "advised" by the "*Gouvernement Général*" to leave Algeria in March 1940, beginning an enforced exile from his roots which will wound him forever.

PARIS 1940

Camus arrives in Paris at the moment of "*la drôle de guerre*", the "phoney war" or military face-off with the demoralized French army entrenched behind the Maginot Line, waiting for the inevitable German onslaught which, when it finally comes, is not where it was supposed to be. The French defences now in ruins, it is only a matter of weeks before Hitler's army enters Paris.

And this is the City of Light which the *pied-noir* Albert Camus – feeling very much "*l'étranger*" – encounters for the first time. "*Paris is dead. The danger is everywhere. You go home and wait for the alert signal or whatever. I get stopped constantly in the street and asked for my ID: charming atmosphere.*"

He hardly has time to start his new job as a reporter for the newspaper *Paris-Soir* when the whole staff is packed off to the town of Clermont-Ferrand and then to the western port of Bordeaux to avoid the Nazis as long as possible. In Camus' suitcase – travelling "light" – a couple of white shirts, his favourite dandy bow-ties, a toothbrush and the "three absurds", manuscripts in varying states of completion.

To elaborate the notion of the **Absurd** – his great and lasting contribution to modern thought – Camus had divided his labours into three parts: a novel (**L'Étranger**), a book of philosophical essays (**Le Mythe de Sisyphe**) and a play (**Caligula**), each informing the other, the fictions playing out the dilemma described in the essays, yet each an "*oeuvre*" unto itself.

The **Absurd** is a much misunderstood philosophical category, primarily due to its sense of linguistic *finality* both in French and English. To use the expression "that's absurd!" brings with it an automatic negative judgement and a feeling that all further discussion is thereby closed.

SUDDENLY THE STAGE SET COLLAPSES. GETTING UP, THE STREETCAR, FOUR HOURS OF OFFICE OR FACTORY, LUNCH, STREETCAR, FOUR HOURS OF WORK, SUPPER, SLEEP AND MONDAY, TUESDAY, WEDNESDAY, THURSDAY, FRIDAY, SATURDAY …

For Camus, "absurdity" is the given premise of all modern experience, an uneasy feeling, above all, a sense of contradiction, and is only the **beginning** of a perception of life, its meaning and consequences. Unlike the German philosopher **Friedrich Nietzsche** (1844-1900) – whose influence on him is considerable – Camus does not need to declare God "dead". God, or any kind of divine "unmoved mover" or guiding hand for human life, does not even come into the picture. Camus simply presumes the absence of any kind of universal logic or direction generally associated with the idea of divinity. He doesn't even miss or desire God. No thanks, I'll find my own way around the labyrinth.

... ALL AT THE SAME RHYTHM — MOST OF THE TIME IT'S EASY TO FOLLOW THIS PATH. BUT ONE FINE DAY THE "WHY" OF IT OVERCOMES US AND EVERYTHING BEGINS IN THAT WEARINESS TAINTED BY ASTONISHMENT.

Without divinity there can be no presumed code of conduct for human beings, nor any explanation of life's meaning. We are simply thrown into this world and the outcome is **death**, pure and simple. There is only life before and nothing beyond. And yet, this absence of explanation is not, in itself, the idea of the Absurd. "*What is absurd is the confrontation between the sense of the irrational and the overwhelming desire for clarity which resounds in the depths of man.*"

I COME AROUND FINALLY TO DEATH AND OUR ATTITUDE TOWARDS IT. EVERYTHING HAS ALREADY BEEN SAID ABOUT THIS AND IT'S ONLY RIGHT TO KEEP PATHOS OUT OF IT. STILL, WE CAN NEVER BE AMAZED ENOUGH THAT EVERYONE LIVES AS IF NOBODY "KNEW".

The Absurd is thus a **pointless quest for meaning** in a universe devoid of purpose. It is a totally human foible and, once again, only defines the **beginning** of the questioning of existence. **Coming to terms with the Absurd** is what essentially concerns Camus, because this accounts for the terrible "*weight and strangeness*" of the world as experienced by every human being. The feeling of absurdity is "*the separation between man and his life*", an actor walking out on stage and not recognizing the scenery or knowing the lines of the play he is supposed to speak, a sense of permanent displacement and un-belonging.

THIS IS BECAUSE, IN REALITY, THERE IS NO EXPERIENCE OF DEATH. CLEARLY, ONLY THAT WHICH HAS BEEN LIVED AND MADE CONSCIOUS CAN BE EXPERIENCED. HERE, IT IS JUST SCARCELY POSSIBLE TO SPEAK OF EXPERIENCING THE DEATH OF OTHERS.

Nowhere is the Absurd more aptly described than in the novel he was carrying in his exile's suitcase. In a notebook of 1938, Camus had scribbled …

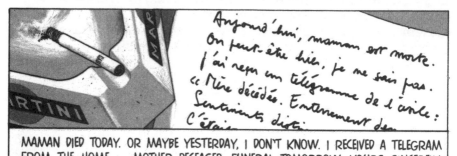

MAMAN DIED TODAY. OR MAYBE YESTERDAY, I DON'T KNOW. I RECEIVED A TELEGRAM FROM THE HOME : MOTHER DECEASED. FUNERAL TOMORROW. YOURS SINCERELY. THAT DOESN'T MEAN A THING. MAYBE IT WAS YESTERDAY.

… which was destined to become one of the most famous first paragraphs in contemporary literature.

The title of Camus' classic novel is difficult to render into English because the French word bears the connotations of both "stranger" and "foreigner" at the same time, and each of these concepts is at play in the novel. Still, **The Stranger** is, by far, the only coherent translation. That generations of English (as opposed to American) readers have known this book by the unfortunate title "The Outsider" is yet another example of misleading translation.

Meursault, the novel's hero, a "stranger" to the system of Christian morality insofar as he cannot comprehend it, is certainly not an "outsider", neither consciously choosing to remain "outside" society nor being rejected by it. On the contrary, Meursault is the perfect model of a young lower-middle-class *pied-noir*, with an ordinary desk job, and with the ordinary **insider's** simple taste for watching a banal film, having a drink at the local bar, going to the beach, lying in the sun (his original name, Mersault, is a pun on the French words *mer* and *soleil*, sea and sun). He is very much **inside** the French Algerian colonial scene, living the most ordinary of lives, not at all a social reject and in **no way a rebel** … at least not yet.

After the embarrassment of having to ask his boss for a day off to attend his mother's funeral, Meursault takes the bus to Marengo, about eighty kilometres from Algiers.

At the old-age home …

MADAME MEURSAULT CAME HERE THREE YEARS AGO.
YOU WERE HER ONLY SUPPORT.

SHE OFTEN EXPRESSED THE DESIRE FOR A RELIGIOUS BURIAL. I'VE MADE ALL THE ARRANGEMENTS.

MY MOTHER NEVER GAVE A THOUGHT TO RELIGION IN ALL HER LIFE.

Then, after a time …

WE'VE ALREADY COVERED HER UP. BUT I'M SUPPOSED TO UNSCREW THE CASKET SO YOU CAN TAKE A LOOK AT HER.

NO.

I DON'T KNOW.

WHY NOT?

Meursault drinks a cup of coffee and smokes a cigarette by the coffin, two innocent gestures which, later, will aid in his downfall.

After an all-night vigil in the presence of Maman's "friends" from the old-age home, Meursault greets the day of his mother's burial with typical Camusian delight at the beauty of Algeria.

ABOVE THE HILLS SEPARATING MARENGO FROM THE SEA, THE SKY WAS BRIGHT RED. AND THE WIND WHICH CAME OVER THE HILLS BROUGHT WITH IT THE SMELL OF SALT.

Meursault would prefer to go for a walk in this landscape, yet he has little choice but to attend the funeral. Exceptionally, one of the old people is allowed to come to the burial. This is Thomas Perez, a close friend of Madame Meursault, called by the others her "*fiancé*". At this point, the punishing sunlight of the countryside begins to make its impact on him.

I FELT LOST BETWEEN THE BLUE AND WHITE OF THE SKY AND THE MONOTONY OF THE COLOURS ALL AROUND ME.

The return journey to Algiers seems almost a relief to him.

Back in Algiers, Meursault decides to go for a swim and runs into an old office acquaintance, Marie Cardona.

They go to the beach together …

… then, in the evening, to see a Fernandel comedy film …

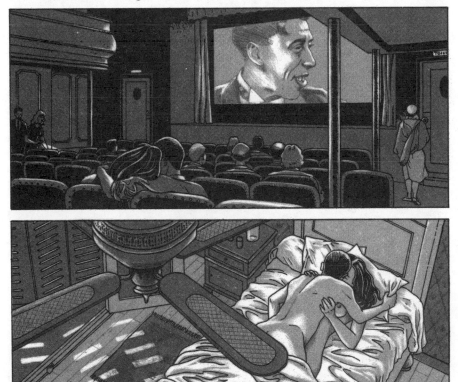

… and then to bed.

The next day, Meursault watches a typical Algiers Sunday roll by from his balcony: trams, moviegoers, football supporters, a scene seemingly full of everyday banality but, in Camus' personal universe, pure delight.

I THOUGHT : ANOTHER SUNDAY GONE, MAMAN BURIED, TOMORROW BACK TO WORK AND, REALLY, NOTHING AT ALL HAS CHANGED.

Nothing has changed, nothing will change, as far as Meursault is concerned. His refrain is: *"cela m'est égal."*

IT'S ALL THE SAME TO ME.

His boss offers him advancement to an office in Paris, but it's all the same to him. In any case: *"You can never change your life, one's as good as another, and anyway, I'm not at all unsatisfied with mine."*

To Marie's suggestion of marriage …

DO YOU LOVE ME?

THEN WHY MARRY ME?

PROBABLY NOT.

IT DOESN'T MAKE ANY DIFFERENCE TO ME.

Meursault meets his neighbour on the stairs, a banal, chance encounter which will ultimately cost him his life. This is Raymond Sintès, local thug and pimp who asks Meursault to draft a letter for him to his "girlfriend". This simple gesture will involve Meursault in a spiral of events over which he has no control, in which he is the leading player and yet a total "stranger". Raymond is known for beating up the "girlfriend" and has already had a scrap with her brother.

Raymond invites Meursault and Marie to spend a day at the seaside with some of his friends. They decide to take the bus. But just in front of a tobacconist's shop …

Camus, who fought all his life for a just society in which the two communities could live in harmony, was never able to make an Arab come alive in his fiction. Here, the scene is typical: "*They watched us silently, but in their special way, no more or no less than if we were stones or dead trees.*" The brother of Raymond's "girlfriend" is amongst them.

They take the bus through the suburbs of Algiers …

… and arrive at the beach-house of Raymond's friend, Masson. Here, Camus makes use of a real incident in his life, which marked him enough to reproduce it as one of the key scenes in **L'Étranger**. On the strand at Bouisseville near Oran, where the beaches were segregated by mutual unspoken consent, one of Camus' friends had a run-in with a group of Arabs which eventually involved a knife, a cut, a revolver, but no one dead. Camus himself was involved in this macho scene, although not in the fight itself.

Transformed into literature …

Now bandaged up and itching for revenge, Raymond goes back to the beach, followed by Meursault. Only this time, there is a new factor: Raymond's revolver. They find the two Arabs again, one playing a flute, at a small spring behind a huge rock. Raymond thinks of shooting his man, but Meursault tells him he can only shoot in self-defence if the Arab pulls his knife. Then he takes Raymond's gun, which the sunlight catches, and goes back with him to the beach house.

But now the incredible heat and **sunlight** become major players in the story. Meursault does not re-enter the cabin, but turns back to the beach, although "*to stay or to go it was all the same thing*".

The inexorable logic of the Algerian sun takes over.

FOR ME, THIS WHOLE BUSINESS WAS FINISHED, AND I HAD COME BACK HERE WITHOUT EVEN THINKING ABOUT IT.

ALL I NEEDED TO DO WAS TO TURN BACK AND IT WOULD BE OVER.

IT WAS THE SAME SUN AS ON THE DAY I BURIED MAMAN.

THE LIGHT SHOT OFF THE STEEL AND IT WAS LIKE A GLEAMING BLADE SLASHING AT MY FOREHEAD. IT SEEMED AS IF THE SKY OPENED UP FROM END TO END TO RAIN DOWN FIRE.

BLAM

THE TRIGGER GAVE WAY... AND IN THAT DRY BUT DEAFENING NOISE EVERYTHING BEGAN. I SHOOK OFF THE SUN AND THE SEA. I REALISED I HAD DESTROYED THE HARMONY OF THE DAY, THE EXCEPTIONAL SILENCE OF A BEACH WHERE I'D BEEN HAPPY.

BLAM BLA LA N

AND IT WAS LIKE FOUR SHORT KNOCKS ON THE DOOR OF UNHAPPINESS.

The second part of **L'Étranger** is completely taken up with Meursault's arrest, arraignment, incarceration, trial and punishment. The world of justice, the courts, the typical two-facedness of lawyers is one to which the hero of Camus' novel is as much a "stranger" as is Josef K. in Kafka's **The Trial**, whose influence is felt here.

Except that, unlike Kafka's K., Meursault doesn't try to understand the meaning of what happens to him. An absurd universe is, above all else, **incomprehensible**. In **Le Mythe de Sisyphe** (**The Myth of Sisyphus**, 1942) Camus would write: "*A world which can be explained, even through bad reasoning, is a familiar one. On the other hand, in a world suddenly devoid of illusion and light, man feels like a stranger.*"

Not having chosen a lawyer, Meursault is assigned one by the court. Meursault is informed that his behaviour at his mother's funeral has been judged "insensitive", and that this will undoubtedly count against him at his trial. The lawyer wants to argue that he was upset and held back his natural feelings, but Meursault refuses this line of defence because it isn't true.

Then, with the examining magistrate …

There follows one of the novel's most famous sequences, as Meursault is put into a cell with a group of Arabs …

The Arabs' response is to help him make up his bed.

With time, Meursault begins to have "*the thoughts of a prisoner*".

I OFTEN THOUGHT THEN THAT IF I HAD BEEN MADE TO LIVE IN THE TRUNK OF A DEAD TREE, WITH NOTHING ELSE TO DO BUT WATCH THE FLOWERING OF THE SKY ABOVE MY HEAD, I WOULD HAVE GROWN USED TO IT LITTLE BY LITTLE.

Meursault is even a spectator/stranger at his own trial. He watches the proceedings with great interest, and is amazed at the way the prosecution twists its case, but always as if **someone else** – and not he – were on trial.

HE DIDN'T WANT TO SEE HIS MOTHER'S CORPSE. HE SMOKED IN THE MORTUARY. HE FELL ASLEEP. HE DRANK A CAFÉ AU LAIT.

OOOHH !

EVEN IN THE DOCK, IT'S ALWAYS INTERESTING ...

... TO HEAR PEOPLE TALKING ABOUT YOU.

In the darkness of the
prison van …

I REDISCOVERED, ONE AFTER THE OTHER : THE CRIES OF THE NEWSPAPER VENDORS, THE LAST BIRDS IN THE PARK, THE CALL OF THE SANDWICH MERCHANTS, THE SCREECH OF THE TRAMS, AND THAT BUZZING IN THE AIR BEFORE THE NIGHT ENVELOPS THE PORT...
YES, IT WAS THE HOUR WHEN, A LONG TIME AGO, I HAD FELT CONTENTMENT.

Now begins Meursault's full realization of what has happened to him, the complete objectification of his person through accusation and judgement, which is, after all, the prelude to his execution.

IN A CERTAIN WAY, MY CASE WAS BEING DEALT WITH AS IF IT DIDN'T CONCERN ME. EVERYTHING HAPPENED WITHOUT MY PARTICIPATION.
MY FATE WAS BEING DECIDED WITHOUT ANYBODY ASKING MY OPINION.

The notions of judgement and retribution are foreign to Meursault. When he is asked if he regrets his action, he realizes that he never "regrets" anything. "*I was always busy with what was happening next, today or tomorrow.*"

HAS THE ACCUSED ANYTHING TO SAY?

I DIDN'T INTEND TO KILL THE ARAB.

WHY DID YOU DO IT?

BECAUSE OF THE SUN.

Meursault is condemned to death by the guillotine, and once again Camus' life-long horror of the death penalty and, in particular, this barbaric French blade from the 18th century, is brought into play. Meursault recounts the author's key trauma of his father witnessing a public execution and being sickened by the sight. Yet his revulsion is not one of outraged non-violence.

IF I EVER GET OUT OF THIS PRISON, I'LL GO AND WATCH ALL PUBLIC EXECUTIONS.

He imagines a new penal code in which the condemned man would be killed by a mixture of chemicals, but in which he would still have a minuscule chance of survival. Whereas, with the guillotine, there is no chance whatsoever. If the blade happened to fail, it would just be sharpened and the execution would begin all over again. In this way, the condemned is forced to hope that it works the first time around, a hope which makes him a **moral accomplice to his own murder**. Which is precisely what is wanted of him: that he consent to his own condemnation, thereby justifying society's need to eliminate him.

Meursault is also fascinated by the sadistic precision of the guillotine, especially its positioning. He is willing to accept the idea of mounting a scaffold, going up towards the sky only to plunge again. But this is not the case.

THE GUILLOTINE IS ON THE SAME LEVEL AS THE MAN WHO APPROACHES IT. HE WALKS UP TO IT AS YOU WOULD WALK UP TO ANOTHER PERSON.

Meursault is on the road to becoming the Absurd Hero, one who will accept the non-sense of the world which has condemned him, not passively, but as a full participant in the brief time left to him. While waiting for his appeal, Meursault begins an "absurd reasoning" and starts to consider his death. He knows there is not so much difference between dying at thirty or seventy. It's still death and there's nothing afterwards, therefore, he has to – logically – reject his own appeal. At the same time, there is a typical Camusian clinging to life: "*At this point my chain of thought was shaken by the terrible leap I felt in me at the idea of having twenty more years to live.*"
Suddenly the prison chaplain, whom Meursault has so far refused to see, arrives …

GOD WILL HELP YOU.

I DON'T HAVE TIME TO WASTE ON GOD. I'M GUILTY, I'M PAYING FOR IT, NOBODY CAN ASK ANY MORE OF ME.

YOUR HEART IS BLIND. I WILL PRAY FOR YOU.

SO SURE OF YOURSELF, ARE YOU ? NONE OF YOUR CERTAINTIES IS WORTH ONE HAIR OF A WOMAN'S HEAD!

FROM SOMEWHERE DEEP IN MY FUTURE, THROUGHOUT THE WHOLE OF THIS ABSURD LIFE I'D LIVED, A DARK WIND WAS MOVING TOWARDS ME ACROSS THE YEARS STILL TO COME.

The calm which comes after this storm of abuse is unlike any other in modern literature. In the final paragraph of *L'Étranger*, Camus does not "sum up" his hero's fate, but leads him into a breathtaking vision of new life in the face of death.

JUST AT THAT MOMENT, AND AT THE FAR END OF THE NIGHT, SIRENS BEGAN TO WAIL. THEY ANNOUNCED DEPARTURES FOR A WORLD WHICH NOW MEANT NOTHING TO ME.

For the first time in ages, he thinks about Maman and understands why she took on a "*fiancé*" in her last years and played at beginning all over again.

And then, purged of his rage and, especially, of all **hope** …

NOBODY, NOBODY HAS THE RIGHT TO CRY OVER HER.

… I OPENED MYSELF FOR THE FIRST TIME TO THE TENDER INDIFFERENCE OF THE WORLD.

Happy in this final acceptance of his own absurdity …

... IT ONLY REMAINED TO WISH MYSELF A LARGE CROWD OF SPECTATORS ON THE DAY OF MY EXECUTION AND THAT THEY WOULD GREET ME WITH CRIES OF HATE.

Like Kafka's *The Trial*, *L'Étranger* has in itself become the subject of countless books, theses, essays, debates, interpretations, making it one of those great works of literature known perhaps as much for what is **said about it** as for what it says.

The focal point of most studies is, of course, the murder itself, an unresolvable enigma which leaves most critics and readers baffled. Rarely is the novel discussed in its social and historical context for the perfectly valid reason that Camus himself only assumes this, and never insists on it. Yet whatever motives can or cannot be ascribed to Meursault's act, there can be no doubt about its basic format. We are in colonial Algeria. **A *pied-noir* kills an Arab**. An Arab he doesn't know, who is scarcely described as a human being and who remains chiefly an abstraction. Can this murder be totally coincidental or is it somehow "written" in the subconscious – a sub-textual acting out of a terrible desired historical ritual – of both the central character and his author?

"*Terrible days lie ahead of us*", Camus wrote from the mainland to a friend in Algeria. In June 1940, the French signed an armistice with Hitler which effectively divided France in two. An "occupied zone", including most territory north of Lyon and the Atlantic coastline, was controlled directly by the Germans. The southern or "non-occupied zone" (disparagingly called the "*Nono*") would be governed from the spa town of Vichy by the ex-World World I hero, Marshal Philippe Pétain, beginning an era of Fascist collaboration which would continue to haunt the French conscience right up to the end of the 20th century and most likely beyond.

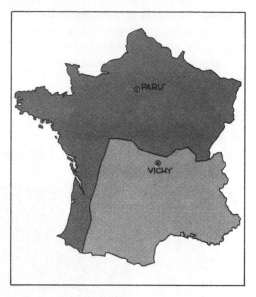

Camus had sized up the new *régime* immediately, with its slogan of "*Travail, Famille, Patrie*" (Work, Family, Country) and its return-to-the-soil ideology: "*A return to the Middle Ages, to a primitive mentality, to the land, to religion, to the whole arsenal of old solutions.*"

In this new atmosphere, few resisted, others collaborated and most people kept their mouths shut and went on with their daily lives. This would continue to be the case even when the Vichy government began handing over Jews to the Nazis, sending them first to what they pretended were only "way-stations", but which were in fact concentration camps, the most famous being that at Drancy in the north of Paris. From here, many were loaded onto cattle cars and transported to Auschwitz.

To a large degree, an aspiring young writer like Camus, as yet unknown in France, would have been expected to collaborate, as did many writers, including the well-known. Yet he refused to write for, or let his work be published in, the *Nouvelle Revue Française* (NRF), edited by the collaborationist author **Pierre Drieu La Rochelle** (1893-1945). At the same time, the *Propaganda Staffel*, the German censor, saw no objection to the "apolitical" novel ***L'Étranger*** being published by the distinguished house of Gallimard.

* "Jews Forbidden."

* "Non-Alcohol Day."

It was in these dark times that Camus put the finishing touches to the next of the "three absurds", *Le Mythe de Sisyphe* (*The Myth of Sisyphus*), certainly one of the most influential books of the mid-20th century. He had been working on it for some five years already, elaborating the philosophical consequences of the Absurd, but there is no doubt that the book is also, in its own way, a reflection of the collapse of the old order in the wake of the Fascist onslaught. For Camus, the relevant question is: how is one to act, without any guiding moral code, in the face of such **massive irrationality**?

Le **M**ythe de **S**isyphe

(The Myth of Sisyphus)

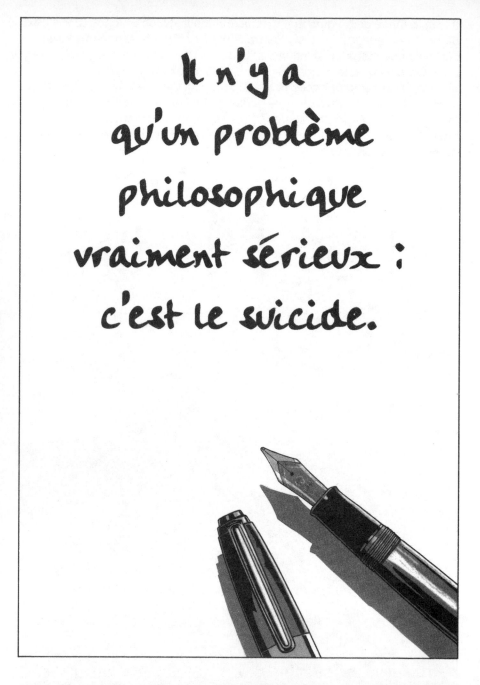

Il n'y a
qu'un problème
philosophique
vraiment sérieux :
c'est le suicide.

"There is only one really serious philosophical problem, and that is suicide."

So begins Camus' essay, with a **BANG** and a *shock*.

If there is no meaning or purpose to life, what's the point of going on? He claims that suicide has always been dealt with as a social problem, whereas for him it is existential, the only question which really counts.

A suicide "*is prepared in the silence of the heart in the same manner as a great work of art*". To die by one's own hand means recognizing "*the lack of any serious reason for living ... and the futility of suffering*".

In the absence of a God or divine "judge", a human being becomes both the accused as well as his own judge and has the right to condemn himself.

And yet, clearly, even those writers who in his estimation have confronted the Absurd – **Søren Kierkegaard** (1813-55), **Feodor Dostoyevsky** (1821-81), **Franz Kafka** (1883-1924), **Edmund Husserl** (1859-1938) etc. – do not take the suicide option and thus become reconciled to the irrational. This leads them, according to Camus, to accept that the human desire for comprehension will be refused and man left in a permanent state of **humiliation**. Camus rejects those philosophers – such as **Karl Jaspers** (1883-1969) and Kierkegaard – who attempt to mystify the Absurd as a means of explaining it away.

It is at this point that Camus' originality becomes evident. It is not by suicide that a human being confronts the Absurd. The point is "*to die unreconciled and not voluntarily. Suicide is a lack of understanding.*" "*Living*", in fact, is a matter of "*keeping the absurd alive. Keeping it alive is basically a question of observing it.*"

Living the Absurd, above all, "*means a TOTAL LACK OF HOPE (which is not the same as despair), a permanent rejection (which is not the same as renunciation), and a conscious dissatisfaction (which is not the same as juvenile anxiety).*"

In this last phrase, Camus is effectively describing Meursault's state of mind while waiting for execution.

Hence the seeming contradiction:

"*Life will be more fully lived IN SO FAR AS IT HAS NO MEANING.*"

In fact, the absence of hope frees the Absurd man from any illusions about the future and he can now "*live out his adventure within the confines of his own lifetime*".

Again, that key word "**ADVENTURE**" for those who cannot see the curious "**OPTIMISM -WITHOUT-HOPE**" in Camus. This side of death, an ultimate freedom reigns.

Camus now unleashes several models to try to describe the actions of Absurd man. These seem rather arbitrary, all aspects of Camus' own personality, more "literary" than "philosophical", rendering this part of his book extremely vague and high-flown.

The first of these is **Don Juan** (Camus is reported to have recognized his own image in Mozart's **Don Giovanni**) who creates for himself "*an ethic of quantity*" rather than quality. He is not fooled by that form of hope known as love. Here the Mediterranean macho in Camus has free rein: "*Nostalgia for desire lost in satisfaction, that commonplace of impotence, does not belong to him.*"

The **actor** is also an Absurd model in that he lives out a multiplicity of lives to the full. In a few short hours of performance time (or longer if he's French or German), "*he travels the whole of the dead end road which his spectator takes a lifetime to cover*". Again, a matter of **quantity**.

Along with the **conqueror** and the **artist**, according to Camus, each of these models knows that his activity is **useless**, is without any future and, knowing this, is able to follow his adventure to the extreme. (One of Camus' primary Absurd heroes is Captain Ahab chasing the white whale in ***Moby-Dick***.) Each in his own way is a prince without a kingdom, "*but having the advantage of knowing that all kingdoms are illusory*". They are "*men who have given up all hope*" and who are endowed with "*a lucid indifference*".

But the ultimate Absurd Hero for Camus (and the centre of perhaps the most original part of his book) is the mythical figure **Sisyphus** who, because of his "*scorn for the gods, his hatred of death and his passion for life*", is condemned by the gods to roll a stone endlessly up to the top of a hill, only to have it roll back down and to start his task all over again. Camus claims to be interested in the moment of "*pause*" when Sisyphus has to go back down the hill, for that's when the **consciousness** of his fate and thus his **acceptance** begins. The author cannot imagine a greater torture for Sisyphus than "*the hope of succeeding*". Knowing that his effort is **pointless** is precisely his strength. Sisyphus is without the merest hope, and yet he becomes the Absurd man the moment he accepts this and "*says yes to his task*", when **he himself chooses** to continue the torture which has been imposed on him. He is master of his own fate. The absence of any controlling force in the universe thus becomes a **positive** factor.

Sisyphus was also, metaphorically, France suffering under the terrible stone-weight of Nazi occupation. At the same time, he is the perfect symbolic hero for Camus in that he attempted to save mankind from Death. "*The struggle itself towards the heights is enough to fill a man's heart. **We have to imagine Sisyphus happy**.*"

No need to commit suicide.

There is a chapter of **Le Mythe de Sisyphe** which does not figure in the original (1943) edition, and which exists as an "appendix" to all post-war editions. This is the chapter called "Hope and the absurd in the work of Franz Kafka". Having to submit all manuscripts to a Nazi control commission, it was clear to Gallimard that **Le Mythe** would never pass the censor with a chapter about a Jewish writer. It is obvious that Camus had to acquiesce in amputating the essay, expressing the hope that somehow it would be published in the "free zone" as part of the entire book (it was not).

Camus would always insist that he was not an Existentialist, even though the publication of **Le Mythe de Sisyphe** put him squarely in that box in the public mind. He would also come to be associated with the notion of the Absurd, even though he did not invent it and would soon go beyond it (without renouncing it). He would say "*it was an idea I found in the streets of our times*". It was for him a "*positive nihilism*", a means of living with the rampant negativity of the era and seeing in it a road to survival.

Having confronted his beast in narrative fiction and also in a philosophical tract, Camus continued his original plan for the three simultaneous "absurds" by placing his theme in a theatrical context. In many ways, the theatre was one of his chief lifetime obsessions and, from his early days in Algiers directing the leftist *Théâtre du Travail*, right up to the end of his life, when he was on the verge of taking over one of Paris' major theatre buildings, he was *un homme de théâtre*. His forte was directing (taking an interest in stagecraft, lighting, etc. as well), and in adapting other authors' work for the stage. His own plays, always challenging, suffer from the same intellectual malaise as much of his fiction: so much to be said, but without the story-teller's master hand or the dramatist's knowing eye. Rarely is he able to perform the playwright's primary task: to step back and let a character assume his own voice and spin his own destiny-web.

GÉRARD PHILIPE AND ALBERT CAMUS DURING A REHEARSAL OF *CALIGULA*.

Yet the third "absurd", the play **Caligula**, written and rewritten and revised and reconsidered numerous times between the late 1930s and late 1950s, stands as a classical dramatic statement if not as a classic play. It is also Camus' most famous stage work, in no small part due to the legendary performance of the great French actor, Gérard Philipe, in the title role in the original production.

38 A.D. The young emperor Caius Caligula, one of the twelve Caesars, experiences the death of his sister and lover, Drusilla. Hit full in the face by the Absurd, he recognizes that "**men die and they are not happy**". Nothing particular here; this is the Absurd hero's obligatory starting-point. With the essential difference that Caligula has **power** over others.

And if the Absurd exists, if "*this world has no importance*", as he says, then it is in his hands as emperor to carry this logic as far as he likes. If the universe is irrational, then he will pursue an ultimate freedom in order to let the irrational reign in his kingdom. If Meursault is the Absurd Hero with no access to the world, Caligula is his almighty anti-face.

The code of conduct now becomes nothing more than Caligula's whim. He kills, copiously, but not necessarily those who have erred or in any way deserve death. He decrees a famine and overturns the state economy, even creating a "national brothel". He continually humiliates his subjects, especially the patricians, rapes their wives, forces the national poets to lick their poems off their slates.

Proving that he can assume the role of the gods, he dresses in drag and forces the patricians to worship him/her. The others finally plot against him and he is aware of their manoeuvres and does not stop them, leading some critics to interpret the play as an elaborate suicide.

In the end he claims to be happy, while strangling his mistress, Caesonia.

CAESONIA, YOU'VE BEEN WATCHING A STRANGE TRAGEDY RIGHT TO ITS END. IT'S TIME TO BRING THE CURTAIN DOWN ON YOU.

THIS IS HAPPINESS, THIS INTOLERABLE RELEASE, THIS UNIVERSAL CONTEMPT, BLOOD, HATRED ALL AROUND ME, THIS UNIQUE ISOLATION OF THE MAN WHO ALL HIS LIFE KNOWS THE BOUNDLESS JOY OF THE UNPUNISHED KILLER, THIS RUTHLESS LOGIC WHICH CRUSHES HUMAN LIVES ...

In the very last instants of the play, Caligula's assassins rush in from all sides, stabbing him from every angle, yet provoking only final scorn from him:

I'M STILL ALIVE !

First performed in 1945, Caligula has invariably been compared to Hitler or his actions at least seen as a mirror to Nazi atrocities. And yet, for the Roman Emperor, nothing so "ordinary" as genocide. *"A tyrant is a man who sacrifices people to his ideals or his ambition. But I have no ideals and I already have all the power I want."* Why, then, all the butchery? To make up for *"the stupidity and hatred of the gods"*.

Caligula is, in some ways, a manifestation of the very Dostoyevskian notion that **if God does not exist, everything is permissible**. During the war, Camus wrote a series of letters to a fictitious German *alter ego*, published clandestinely in 1943 under the title **Lettres à un ami allemand** (**Letters to a German Friend**). These letters both mirror and challenge many of the ideas in **Caligula** and form an important **pivot** in Camus' thinking, away from the Absurd as an absolute and towards his later, more complex political positions.

> EVEN WHILE JUDGING YOUR ATROCIOUS BEHAVIOUR, I WILL RECALL THAT YOU AND I STARTED OUT FROM THE SAME SOLITUDE.

Both he and the "friend" believe that the world is not governed by a superior intelligence and he, Camus, reiterates his belief in this absence, using familiar "absurdist" language.

> I KNOW THAT THE SKY WHICH WAS INDIFFERENT TO YOUR HORRIBLE VICTORIES WILL STILL BE SO AT YOUR JUST DEFEAT.

Yet, if both have begun from the standpoint of **despair,** the "friend" has taken the road to mass murder while he, Camus, finds his comfort in human **solidarity**. One has chosen to take his revenge on an indifferent universe, the other chooses **justice** and fidelity to the earth, even while continuing to believe in the futility of existence.

> EVERY MUTILATION OF A HUMAN BEING IS IRREVERSIBLE.

In the "Letters", Camus attributes a certain "purity" to France and the French in the face of World War II, even promoting the self-justifying myth that they held back from fighting the Germans in 1940 so as not to add "*to the world's horrible suffering*". Nowhere in the book is the merest hint that many Frenchmen were **pleased** to play supporting roles in the Nazi Epic of fire and blood, and that much of Camus' invective might just as easily have been addressed to *un ami français.*

Still, there is no questioning his anti-Fascist commitment, and from 1942 onwards he found himself in the French resistance group known as …

combat

Camus was not about to take up weapons and rush to the *maquis* where an armed movement was slowly taking shape after two years of German occupation. But he was ready to fight in his own way, as a writer and man of communication.

The *Combat* group was founded in 1942, basically for intelligence-gathering and sabotaging of German military compounds. But from its inception, it distinguished itself from the more conservative resistance movement led by General de Gaulle in London. *Combat* saw the liberation of France as only the beginning of its struggle, and hoped for sweeping political changes afterwards.

Camus was brought into *Combat* under the *nom de guerre* …

BEAUCHARD.

But he played a very small role in its activities until joining the staff of its underground newspaper in October 1943.

Extraordinary measures had to be taken to prevent the paper from falling into the hands of the Gestapo. Pages would be made up and reproduced in reduced format and put onto zinc plates which would then be distributed to various clandestine printers throughout France.

The next hurdle would be to get the printed paper out to the public. A valise full of copies would be sent by train from Lyon, then collected at the Gare de Lyon in Paris by someone pretending to be its owner. Afterwards, copies were shipped in crates to false addresses with fake labels like "cleaning supplies" or something equally innocuous.

In time, Albert Camus was to become the *Combat* group's most famous member, especially following the liberation of France. Suddenly, the father of the Absurd, the visionary of a pointless universe, was risking his life for a **Cause**. Even the simple printing of a leaflet could lead to arrest and deportation, or torture at the hands of the Gestapo and its volunteer French henchmen known as *La Milice* (The Militia).

Camus now received a set of false identity papers …

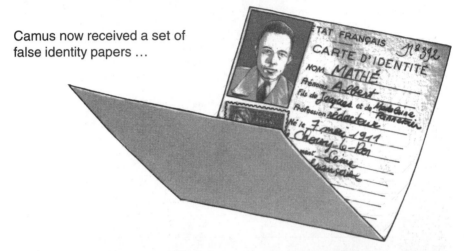

Once, carrying the new masthead for *Combat*, Camus was caught in a street roundup, along with the actress Maria Casarès.

With the Normandy landings in the summer of 1944, the *Résistance* began preparing the liberation of Paris in expectation of the arrival of Allied forces. The movement gained courage and proved to be a real annoyance in case of a necessary German retreat. Collaborators were lynched in the street or summarily shot.

* "Responsible for her husband being shot."

Snipers began picking off German soldiers from rooftops and armed battles raged throughout the city, which usually led to reprisals against the civilian population. This was part of an already mounting face-off between the Communist left, demanding out-and-out insurrection, and de Gaulle's forces calling for moderation.

This was also the beginning of another lovely myth – or half-myth – promulgated by de Gaulle and all the resistance forces (including *messieurs les journalistes de Combat*), that France and Paris had been liberated primarily by **Frenchmen**, with a grudging nod over their shoulders at those Yanks and Brits who just happened to turn up at the same time.

The *Combat* group had already moved from Lyon to Paris, preparing to publish in the capital. With the Allies at the gates of the city, the journalists took over a building which had housed the Nazi newspaper *Pariser Zeitung* during the Occupation. As a reminder of military reality, the staff found cases of hand grenades left behind in the building.

The first Paris issue with its famous sub-title – "*De la Résistance à la Révolution*" – bore a powerful anonymous editorial on its front page.

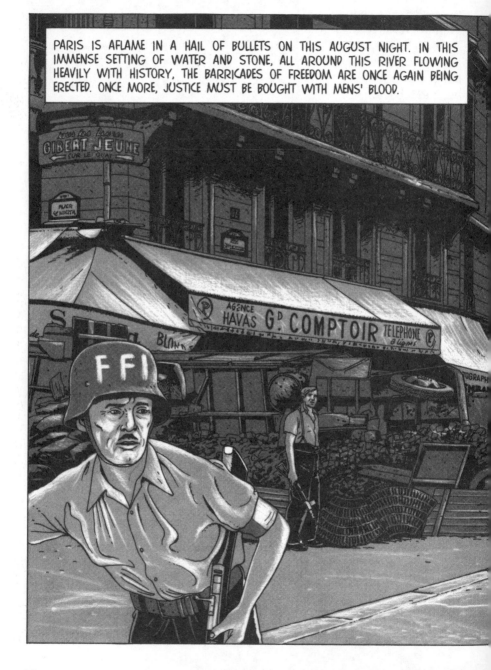

PARIS IS AFLAME IN A HAIL OF BULLETS ON THIS AUGUST NIGHT. IN THIS IMMENSE SETTING OF WATER AND STONE, ALL AROUND THIS RIVER FLOWING HEAVILY WITH HISTORY, THE BARRICADES OF FREEDOM ARE ONCE AGAIN BEING ERECTED. ONCE MORE, JUSTICE MUST BE BOUGHT WITH MENS' BLOOD.

Its obvious literary quality betrayed the identity of its author …

IT IS UNIMAGINABLE THAT MEN WHO FOR FOUR YEARS HAVE FOUGHT IN SILENCE AND IN WHOLE DAYS OF BOMBARDMENTS AND GUNFIRE WILL AGREE TO SEE THE FORCES OF RESIGNATION AND INJUSTICE RETURN IN ANY FORM WHATSOEVER.

NOTHING IS GIVEN TO MAN, AND THE LITTLE WHICH IS HIS TO CONQUER IS PAID FOR BY UNJUST DEATHS. BUT THAT ISN'T WHERE HIS GREATNESS LIES. IT LIES IN HIS DECISION TO BE STRONGER THAN HIS CONDITION. AND IF HIS CONDITION IS UNJUST, HE HAS ONLY ONE MEANS TO RISE ABOVE IT, AND THAT IS FOR HE HIMSELF TO BE JUST.

WE CANNOT LIVE FOREVER BY MURDER AND VIOLENCE. HAPPINESS, TENDERNESS WILL HAVE THEIR DAY. BUT PEACE WILL NOT ALLOW US TO FORGET. AND THERE ARE THOSE AMONG US FOR WHOM THE IMAGE OF OUR BROTHERS MUTILATED BY SHELLS, THE GREAT VIRILE BROTHERHOOD OF THESE PAST YEARS, WILL NEVER LEAVE US.

"The great virile brotherhood" had also found its way into Camus' fiction. In the midst of his *Combat* editorials, he was also completing a new novel which would, through an elaborate metaphor, cover the same political and emotional ground.

With the Allied landings in North Africa in November 1942, Camus had found himself cut off from Algeria, from his mother and his new wife, condemned to indefinite exile in Vichy France. In the central French city of Saint-Etienne, he suffered from his tuberculosis, from the cold as well as the coldness of Europe. The ugly typical spectacle caused him to long for Algiers.

"No population can live without beauty. It can only survive for a while and no longer. And this Europe which shows one of its most persistent faces here distances itself ceaselessly from beauty."

In 1943, when the Nazis invaded the so-called "Zone Libre", effectively taking control of the southern half of France as well as the north, Camus had described their entry as being "*comme des rats*" (like rats).

And rats are indeed the central image of the beginning of his classic novel …

Oran, the Algerian city on the Mediterranean where Camus himself lived briefly, is described as the most "ordinary" of towns, one *"without pigeons, without trees or gardens … a neutral place"*.

We're in the realm of Greek Tragedy. The City is, in effect, the central character of the "chronicle", and its collective fate at the hands of ravaging nature is its spiritual centre.

Camus, of course, makes no secret that "Oran" is a metaphor for occupied France, cut off from civilization by the Nazi plague. But it is also the ultimate testing of human solidarity anywhere, in the face of mass death.

AT LEAST, WE DON'T HAVE ANY DISORDER HERE...

There is no protagonist as such in **La Peste**, and no one undergoes a major spiritual transformation in the course of its inexorable logic. There is only a series of characters, of varying importance, thrown together because of the novel's theme, but scarcely representative of what might be called a "story" with interwoven "intrigues". Typically, for Camus, this group is 100% male and 100% European. In this "Algerian" city – aside from a passing reference to an inquiry into its sanitary conditions – there does not seem to be the merest trace of an Arab population.

ON THE MORNING OF 16 APRIL, DR. BERNARD RIEUX LEFT HIS OFFICE AND CAME UPON A DEAD RAT LYING IN THE MIDDLE OF THE LANDING.

These dead rats will multiply at an alarming rate, leading inevitably to the first human death, that of the *concierge* in Rieux's building.

Yet the most difficult task is to use the word "plague", which, officially, means admitting its existence and having to face the consequences of this admission. Rieux is summoned before the health commission at the prefecture …

TELL ME THE TRUTH : ARE YOU SURE IT'S THE PLAGUE ?

IT ISN'T A QUESTION OF VOCABULARY. IT'S A QUESTION OF TIME.

The next day, the authorities put up little notices around town, taking certain primary measures, but these are hardly sufficient for Rieux. He realizes that they do not "*want to upset public opinion*". Rieux goes to see the government clerk Grand who recounts "*a curious incident at the tobacconist's*" … The tobacconist tells him of a recent case of a young clerk arrested for killing an Arab on a beach.

Cottard, the fugitive from justice, also picks up this theme, discussing a novel he has been reading …

Meanwhile, with daily life taking its ordinary route, the plague becomes almost a "normal" part of it. Spring has come to Oran.

But there is no longer any question of masking its serious nature …

* "DECLARE STATE OF PLAGUE. CLOSE THE CITY."

Once the gates of the city are closed upon its inhabitants, the plague becomes "everyone's concern", even those who have refused to admit its existence or to call it by its rightful name. Like taking sides in Vichy France, it becomes a moral issue of great urgency: fight against the disease with all necessary means or be resigned to its inevitability.

* "French Republic: Public Decree. State of Plague Declared. City Closed."

With Oran now cut off from the rest of the world, the public decrees regarding the plague become draconian. No one is permitted to enter or leave the city under any circumstance, and all mail is forbidden for fear of spreading contagion. Crowds gather at the train station, hoping somehow to escape.

The citizens of Oran are virtual "prisoners" now, forced to live on memory alone. The Port of Oran is deserted. Trains no longer come and go and the only way to deal with this "enforced holiday" is to "*make them run by imagination*". Worse, the continual presence of suffering leads them, unwillingly, to "consent" to the presence of the disease, just as Meursault is supposed to "consent" to his own execution.

Curiously – and extremely French – the cinemas remain full, even though, after a time, the same film is projected over and over again.

With the coming of summer, the city takes on the allure of a prison camp.

* "Prison sentence for anyone attempting to leave the city."   * "Closed due to plague."

* "Drinking wine kills microbes."   * "No more coffee."

On the public streetcars, people keep their distance to avoid contagion.

If Rieux represents the practical side of Camus, the character of Tarrou is more or less his social conscience, in perpetual rebellion against the forces of Thanatos (Death). And yet, in many ways, the two are interchangeable, engaged in the same fight, soul brothers whom the writer Albert Camus is hard pressed to distinguish one from the other. Their "debates" are really no more than those taking place inside the author himself.

Recognizing that the authorities have "no imagination" for dealing with the plague, Tarrou offers Rieux his services …

I'VE DEVELOPED A PLAN FOR CREATING VOLUNTEER HEALTH GROUPS.

THIS WORK CAN BE DEADLY. HAVE YOU REALLY THOUGHT IT OVER ?

Deciding to fight the plague through the new solidarity of mutual work, Camus extends his original metaphor to include the *Résistance* against the Nazi occupation. His work on the underground newspaper *Combat* parallels his private writing of **La Peste**, and there came a point where many paragraphs of his combative articles were lifted from the novel or vice-versa.

La Peste would later become the subject of political polemic: Was "solidarity" or good will enough to fight against human evil? Was this "Red-Cross" mentality really a solution to Fascism?

And, in effect, in defining Nazi inhumanity in terms of a "natural" plague, wasn't "resistance" just an empty slogan, confusing torturers with bacilli?

Camus effectively eliminates all real **opposition** to the Worthy Fight. Indeed, in this monumental work, the only real conflict is between men and the plague. Amongst the characters themselves, all real differences are ironed out or simply discarded by a Camus who is often a great writer but rarely a good **storyteller**.

All funeral services are suspended and, in their place, mass gravesites filled with quicklime.

Once the graves become overcrowded, however, the authorities are forced to use the crematoria. Here, Camus leaves no doubt whatever as to the historical reference, even though many of his compatriots at the time claimed to have been ignorant of the existence of the Nazi death-chambers.

More macabre still …

The streetcars, no longer in public use, had *"their interiors adapted to new purposes, their seats removed, and a line now went directly to the crematorium, its terminus. … And each night, strange convoys of streetcars without travellers passed, rattling along above the sea."*

Confronted with the supremacy of death, the inhabitants of the city, resigned now to their fate, begin a *"long sleep"*, in which they *"resemble nothing at all"* and where the plague has erased *"all value judgements"*, all illusions and, chiefly, memory.

With the autumn comes the new pulmonary form of the plague, and here Camus recognizes his own body at risk. As if to carry his own personal baggage into his grand metaphor, he turns a beloved football stadium into, in effect, a concentration camp/infirmary. This is most certainly a reference to the famous *Vélodrome d'Hiver* in Paris, where thousands of Jews were rounded up in 1942 before being deported to Auschwitz via the Drancy camp.

SUDDENLY, THE LOUDSPEAKERS WHICH, IN BETTER TIMES, ANNOUNCED THE MATCH RESULTS OR INTRODUCED THE TEAMS, DIRECTED THE INTERNEES TO RETURN TO THEIR TENTS FOR THE DISTRIBUTION OF THE EVENING MEAL.

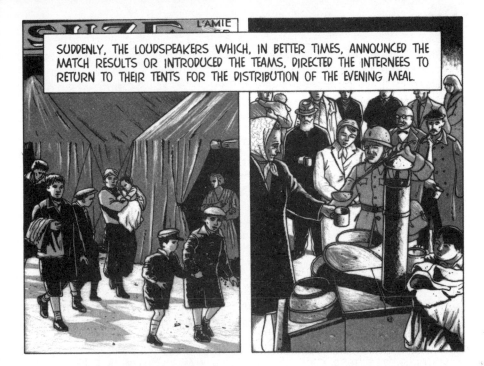

Followed by …

THERE ALSO WERE SEVERAL OTHER CAMPS IN THE CITY, ABOUT WHICH THE NARRATOR, DUE TO DISCRETION AND LACK OF CONCRETE INFORMATION, CAN'T SAY ANY MORE. ALL HE IS ABLE TO SAY IS THAT THE VERY EXISTENCE OF THESE CAMPS, THE SMELL OF THE MEN COMING FROM THEM, THE HUGE BOOM OF THE LOUD-SPEAKERS IN THE TWILIGHT … WEIGHED HEAVILY ON OUR PEOPLE AND ADDED TO THE GENERAL UNEASINESS AND CONFUSION.

The bond between Tarrou and Rieux now tightens enough for Tarrou/ Camus to deliver to Rieux/Camus (once more) the devastating scene where his father tells of witnessing a public execution. Here, in the midst of **mass death**, Camus is again able to step forward and reason against capital punishment, the state's elimination of **one single man**, which he calls the "most abject of all murders". Again, the macabre details horrify and fascinate him …

Tarrou speaks pure Camus when he declares: "*I refuse everything which, for good reasons or bad, leads to death or justifies putting someone to death.*"

And, as if to sanctify their union, Camus leads the two friends to a sacred act – a nocturnal swim – in a mythical place: the Algerian Mediterranean.

This major scene has been interpreted in many ways, some critics even stressing (unnecessarily) its obvious homosexuality which is chiefly fraternal. Yet its meaning is also deeply personal for the author who, in this, the only scene of peace in the entire novel, marries the two conflicting parts of himself …

FOR SEVERAL MINUTES THEY MOVED FORWARD IN THE SAME RHYTHM AND WITH THE SAME VIGOUR, SOLITARY, FAR FROM THE WORLD, FREE AT LAST FROM THE CITY AND FROM THE PLAGUE...

By the end of the year, live rats are seen again in the alleyways and this is taken as a sign of ultimate deliverance from the plague.

Life slowly returns to Oran and, curiously, it is at this point that Tarrou begins to weaken.

I DON'T WANT TO DIE AND I'LL STRUGGLE AGAINST IT. BUT IF I LOSE THE FIGHT, I WANT TO GO DOWN WELL.

NO. TO BECOME A SAINT, YOU HAVE TO LIVE. KEEP FIGHTING.

ONCE MORE THE PLAGUE APPEARED WHERE NO ONE EXPECTED IT, OVERTURNING ALL THE STRATEGIES MOUNTED AGAINST IT. ONCE AGAIN, IT DID ITS BEST TO AMAZE US.

After Tarrou's death, Rieux receives a telegram informing him that his wife, who had left before the arrival of the plague, has also died in her far off sanatorium. He takes this news with "calm".

Finally, the gates of the city re-open. There is dancing in the public squares.

The plague is quickly forgotten by those who simply want to return to their old lives, like those who would oppose the famous "purification" which was to come at the end of the war in France.

Rieux admits to having been the "secret narrator" of the chronicle all along, having done so in order to keep his personal life separate from what is supposed to be objective commentary. He watches as life returns to "normal" …

… but he alone knows what the crowd does not, "*that the plague bacillus never dies or disappears, that it can remain dormant for decades in furniture and bedding, can wait patiently in rooms, in cellars, in trunks, in handkerchiefs and paper, and that perhaps the day would come when, just to teach men a lesson and make them unhappy, the plague would awaken its rats and send them off to die in some happy city.*"

La Peste, published in 1947, was destined to be, in his lifetime, Camus' most popular book, even becoming something of a best-seller in France, prompting its author to quip that the "plague" had taken more victims than he'd ever imagined.

The author **Roland Barthes** (1915-80) saw in the novel the beginning of Camus' period of solitude. But more to the point, after the war: "*Camus' world is one of friends, not of militants.*" In his reply to Barthes, Camus said: "*If there is an evolution from L'Étranger to La Peste, it can be found in the feeling of solidarity and participation.*" **Solidarity**, **participation**, **reconciliation**. Keywords for the post-war Camus who, before the age of 40, would become a kind of "elder statesman" in France, and for whom reconciliation would henceforth outweigh militancy.

This new "conservatism" on Camus' part was not without its ironies and contradictions. He was, after all, still editor of *Combat*, which had declared that liberated France must no longer be in the hands of monied forces, and which had replaced the word "resistance" with "revolution". But his position – often attacked at the time – is not so easy to assess, and has been the subject of much misunderstanding. Camus had always been in the tradition of the great French humanists, and his own childhood had prepared him for a world outlook far different to that of the left-wing Paris intellectual *élite.* The suffering he had seen in the war left him with no doubt that some of his earlier thinking would need revision, but closer analysis shows a moral consistency going right back to his earliest journalistic essays in favour of the Algerian underdog.

While most other European journalists and writers stayed silent or welcomed the horrific American method of ending the war with Japan on 6 August 1945, Camus was crystal clear …

MECHANIZED CIVILIZATION HAS JUST REACHED ITS HIGHEST DEGREE OF SAVAGERY.... THERE IS A CERTAIN INDECENCY IN CELEBRATING A DISCOVERY WHICH ABOVE ALL SERVES THE GREATEST RAGE FOR DESTRUCTION MAN HAS KNOWN FOR CENTURIES.

The business of re-making France was now in the hands of Charles de Gaulle, as head of a tripartite government including Communists and Socialists, which would eventually lead to a Fourth French Republic (de Gaulle would resign in 1946). Inflation was high, rationing in force, the black market thriving, power cuts were the order of the day. Coal and wood for heating were scarce, but so was flour, leading many *boulangeries* to close up shop, a national tragedy.

At the same time, the country was coming out of its Occupation torpor. American soldiers had brought three gifts from which France would never recover: jazz, chewing gum and Coca-Cola.

French women, treated chiefly as sex objects before the war and as brooding-hens for the Fatherland under Pétain, were given the vote for the first time.

At the Café Flore on the Boulevard St. Germain on Paris' Left Bank, the philosopher-playwright-novelist **Jean-Paul Sartre** (1905-80) and the writer **Simone de Beauvoir** (1908-86) would hold court and, even before the end of the war, Camus had become part of their famous *entourage*.

Camus' friendship with the author of ***L'Être et le Néant*** (***Being and Nothingness***, 1943) has often led to the miscalculation that he was, like Sartre, an "Existentialist", and their names are invariably linked. True, there was a great deal uniting them: a brutal world freed from any notion of divinity; the idea of freedom surmounting a basic despair; solidarity as the overriding social value. They were also good mates, good drinking and arguing companions, but time would reinforce their ideological differences, soon leading to one of the most scathing intellectual polemics of modern times.

For a France which had been divided by resistance to, and collaboration with, the Nazis for over four years, one of the most pressing social problems was to root out those who fell into the latter category. At the moment of liberation, this was achieved through uncontrolled acts of vengeance, with nearly 10,000 "*collabos*" summarily lynched or executed by resistance fighters.

THE TRIAL OF MARSHAL PÉTAIN, IN 1945

The more official form was known as "*l'épuration*" (purification or purge) and would prove to be no easy task. Out-and-out traitors like the Vichy Prime Minister Pierre Laval were executed by firing squad and others condemned by special courts and given prison sentences. Marshal Pétain himself was sentenced to death, at a trial attended by Albert Camus, but de Gaulle could not imagine that the French would accept this and, three days later, he pardoned the World War I hero, now well over 80.

But there was a large grey area covering the question of who collaborated and who didn't, and fifty years on, France has not completely come to grips with this problem. Those who could sniff the changing wind in 1943, like the later French President François Mitterrand, quickly turned their Vichy coats inside out and joined the Resistance. Others, like the Bordeaux sub-prefect Maurice Papon, responsible for delivering trainloads of Jews to the Gestapo, patched together faked "resistance" identities, and were taken into the new government as patriotic functionaries. In fact, most of the 11,000 civil servants who had served the Fascists were given their jobs back under de Gaulle, who needed them to help rebuild the country.

For Camus, "*l'épuration*" presented a special problem. Many of France's most famous writers – **Paul Claudel** (1868-1955), **Drieu la Rochelle** (1893-1945), **Charles Maurras** (1868-1952), **Louis-Ferdinand Céline** (1894-1961), **Robert Brasillach** (executed in 1945) and others – had, to some degree, collaborated with or openly supported the Vichy *régime*.

A WINDOW DISPLAY OF ANTI-SEMITIC BOOKS, PARIS - 1941

As opposed to the Catholic novelist **François Mauriac** (1885-1970) who argued for charity, Camus insisted that those who collaborated must face justice. He was pitiless in his demand for the most severe penalty for Pétain. And yet, he quickly saw that very often "*l'épuration*" masked a political agenda, settling old scores or the desire to eliminate political opponents.

But more to the point, Camus simply could not reconcile the need for justice with his lifelong hatred of the death penalty. In a scene somewhat reminiscent of his father's witnessing a guillotining, Camus attended the trial of a collaborator who was surely guilty in his eyes. He left before the end because he suddenly felt himself to be on the side of the accused: "*In every guilty man, there is some innocence. This makes every absolute condemnation revolting.*"

To the journalist Albert Camus, the post-Liberation *Combat* provided the opportunity for a new political morality as well as a new kind of newspaper. He demanded "*a clear and virile press, using respectable language*", one which would not seek to reduce itself to the lowest common denominator. *Combat* counted amongst its contributors some of the great names in French literature – Sartre, de Beauvoir, **André Gide** (1869-1951), **André Malraux** (1901-76) – and managed to keep free of any dogmatic political line.

The paper was well-written, using a new kind of concision which French journalism had not known before. Its stated goal for a new kind of press was "*energy rather than hate, proud objectivity instead of rhetoric, humanity not mediocrity*" .

In one of its celebrated issues, *Combat* reported on the fall of the city of Metz to the Allies, while all other French papers headlined the triumphal entry of Marlene Dietrich into the same city, this already setting Camus apart from what would become journalism's debased wave of the future. The disillusion would not be long in coming. Later, in 1957, long after he had left *Combat*, which had fallen into private hands, he would write: "*This press, which we hoped would be proud and dignified, is today the shame of this unhappy country*."

The early *Combat* made a serious effort to eliminate class and work distinctions between its editorial staff and its print workers. Camus himself later said that he preferred working directly on the metal type to writing editorials, loved the smell of the print room and its *ambiance*.

Although he bemoaned the fact that newspaper work was hurried and that he had no time for serious revision of his articles, Camus considered the *métier* to be as noble as that of novelist or playwright. The journalist was "*a day to day historian*". What's more, Camus could and did reach hundreds of thousands more readers than through his literary work, for a time becoming the most famous journalist in France, and some of his best-known political writings, later incorporated or revised as chapters in his books, began life as *Combat* articles.

In his post-war editorials can be found the development of the second most important word and concept in the Camus canon after "absurd":

LA RÉVOLTE

Camus would never renounce his formulation of the Absurd. For him, the world was still a closed-off "indifferent" place without apparent solace. But moving on from the feeling of individual *Angst* associated with absurd and Existential philosophy, he now poses a new question: "*Can man, alone and without divine help, create his own sense of values?*"

In his essay "*Remarque sur la révolte*" (*Comment on Revolt*, 1945), which would eventually be integrated into the book ***L'Homme Révolté***, 1951 (known in English as ***The Rebel***), Camus indicates the road he has taken in arriving at his post-war thinking.

IN THE ABSURD EXPERIENCE, THE TRAGEDY IS AN INDIVIDUAL ONE. BUT WITH THE MOVEMENT OF REVOLT, THIS TAKES ON A COLLECTIVE AWARENESS.
THE TRAGEDY BECOMES THE ADVENTURE OF EVERYONE...

THE NEGATIVITY WHICH ONE MAN HAS EXPERIENCED UP TO NOW BECOMES A COLLECTIVE PLAGUE.

The idea of *la révolte* develops simultaneously with the increasing distance Camus will take from the post-war Communist movement and its legions of fellow-travellers. For him, "revolution" would become inseparable from the grim visage of Stalinism, and it is as if he needs – almost viscerally now – to change **in his mind**, if not actually on the *Combat* masthead, this word to "revolt"...

REVOLUTION IS NOT REVOLT. IT WAS REVOLT WHICH BOLSTERED THE RESISTANCE FOR FOUR YEARS. IT WAS THE COMPLETE, OBSTINATE REFUSAL, ALMOST BLIND AT THE BEGINNING, OF AN ORDER WHICH WANTED TO BRING MEN TO THEIR KNEES. REVOLT STEMS FIRST OF ALL FROM THE HEART. BUT A TIME COMES WHEN IT PASSES TO THE SPIRIT, WHERE FEELING BECOMES IDEA, WHERE SPONTANEOUS FERVOUR LEADS TO DIRECT ACTION. THIS IS THE MOMENT OF REVOLUTION.

With uncanny foresight of later historical debates in France and elsewhere, he begins his "*Remarque sur la révolte*" with the image of a civil servant refusing to obey an order because he suddenly becomes aware that his superior has gone too far. In doing so, he not only affirms his own integrity, but he is also refusing, rebelling on behalf of the **collective**. Moreover – a particularly Camusian touch – if a slave says "no", he does so not merely *against* his master, but *for* his master as well. Revolt creates a consciousness of **human solidarity**, with a built-in sense of justice and freedom. Obviously, in his pre-Cold War thinking, this pure state of revolt is necessarily **betrayed** in the state of revolution.

Just as he had done with the Absurd, Camus intended to pursue the idea of Revolt through a philosophical work (***L'Homme Révolté***), a novel (***La Peste***) and the play which would come to be known as ...

LES JUSTES

* This title is translated into English as either ***The Just*** or ***The Just Assassins***. Although this latter has a better ring to it, it immediately puts into doubt the main characters' contention that they are dispensers of justice and *not* assassins.

Giving rein to his fascination with the Russian terrorist *milieu* (he would later return to this in his adaptation of Dostoyevsky's **The Possessed**), Camus borrowed an actual event from Moscow in 1905, the bombing assassination of the Grand Duke Sergei Alexandrovitch, uncle of Tsar Nicholas II, and he even used the real historical name of his hero, Kaliayev.

The small band of terrorists, Dora Doulebov, Annenkov, Voinov, dedicated not so much to political overthrow as to bringing justice to all Russians, are mostly typical revolutionary romantics. They are not hardened killers, and Camus even referred to them as "*les meurtriers délicats*" (delicate murderers). They are full of self-doubt and – classically – love of death and self-sacrifice, and in many ways prefigure the *bourgeois* terrorists of the 1970s: the Red Brigades, the German Red Army Faction, the Weathermen in the United States, etc.
Kaliayev, more poet than revolutionary, has been designated to throw the first bomb.

Some nights later (and well offstage) …

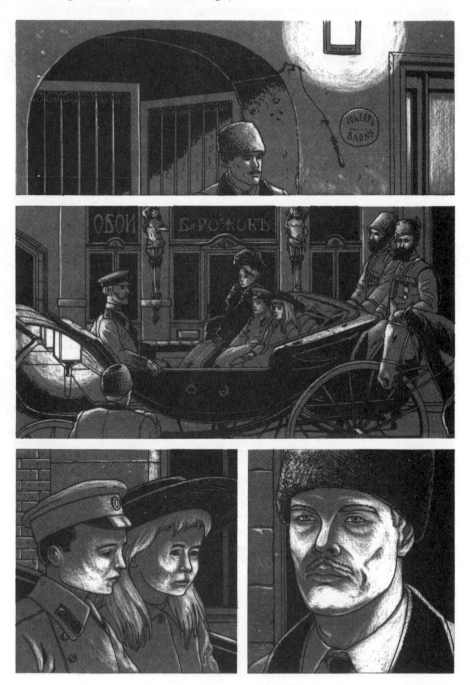

Unable to throw his bomb because of the unexpected presence of the Grand Duke's niece and nephew in the coach, Kaliayev has to render accounts to the rest of the group …

I COULDN'T HAVE FORESEEN.

CHILDREN, CHILDREN ABOVE ALL. DID YOU SEE THE CHILDREN?

THEY WEREN'T LAUGHING. THEY WERE SITTING UPRIGHT IN THE COACH, STARING AT NOTHING IN PARTICULAR. THEY LOOKED SO SAD!

MY ARM BECAME WEAK. MY LEGS WERE TREMBLING.

In the historical accounts of the event of 1905, all other members of the group agreed with Kaliayev's decision not to kill the children. Camus, however, introduces the purely fictional character, Stepan Fedorov, who has suffered torture in the Tsarist prisons, a prototype "Stalinist", for whom the distinction between renderer of justice and assassin is unimportant.

COULD YOU SHOOT A CHILD AT POINT BLANK, STEPAN, WITH YOUR EYES OPEN?

I COULD IF THE ORGANIZATION COMMANDED IT.

This argument now becomes the political crux of the play. If Tarrou had rejected **all** killing for **any** reason in *La Peste*, Camus was able to accept the necessary attaining of justice for limited immediate goals. But he drew the line at the inhuman extremist position that the end justifies all violent means.

OPEN YOUR EYES AND SEE THAT THE ORGANIZATION WOULD LOSE ITS POWER AND INFLUENCE IF, FOR ONE SECOND, IT TOLERATED CHILDREN BEING BLOWN UP BY OUR BOMBS.

WHEN WE DECIDE TO FORGET ABOUT CHILDREN, WE'LL BE MASTERS OF THE WORLD AND THE REVOLUTION WILL TRIUMPH.

AND IF ALL HUMANITY REJECTS THE REVOLUTION ? IF THE PEOPLE YOU'RE FIGHTING FOR REFUSE TO LET CHILDREN BE KILLED ? WILL YOU ATTACK THEM TOO ?

YES, IF NECESSARY, UNTIL THEY'RE MADE TO UNDERSTAND.

After a second attempt to carry out the assassination, Camus makes the task easy for Kaliayev by sending the Grand Duke out alone, without his nephew and niece. He is blown to bits and Kaliayev arrested.

Camus now employs another historical incident, the visit of the Grand Duchess to her husband's murderer in prison, in some ways reminiscent of the scene between Meursault and the prison chaplain at the end of *L'Étranger*. By a curious turn of romantic revolutionary logic (which Camus appears to support), Kaliayev believes that being executed for his act expiates the murder he has committed. Paying with his own life – a kind of calculated revolutionary suicide – is his means of justifying what is normally unjustifiable for Camus, i.e. murder.

DON'T YOU WANT TO PRAY WITH ME, TO REPENT ?

LET ME PREPARE TO DIE. IF I DIDN'T DIE, THEN I'D BE A MURDERER.

DIE ? YOU WANT TO DIE ? NO. YOU MUST LIVE AND FACE UP TO BEING A MURDERER. DIDN'T YOU KILL SOMEONE ? GOD WILL JUSTIFY YOU.

Finally …

I'LL DEMAND PARDON FOR YOU.

I BEG YOU NOT TO DO IT. LET ME DIE OR I'LL HATE YOU FOREVER.

In the final scene, the other terrorists wait for news of Kaliayev's execution, hoping that he doesn't repent. Typically, the grim details are discussed.

> DO YOU KNOW HOW THEY HANG SOMEONE ? THE HANGMAN JUMPS ON HIS SHOULDERS. THE NECK BREAKS...

When news of the execution is brought, Kaliayev is no longer a "murderer" in their eyes and they can continue their revolutionary road with consciences cleared for … suicidal death. Dora, who has up to now only made and set the bombs in motion, asks to be the next to throw one at a reactionary target, even if this goes against the Organization's rule of keeping women out of the front lines.

> YOU'LL GIVE IT TO ME, WON'T YOU ? I'LL THROW IT. AND LATER, ON SOME COLD NIGHT... THE SAME ROPE ! EVERYTHING WILL BE EASIER FROM NOW ON.

Despite its melodramatic nature, **Les Justes** has a real theatrical nobility reminiscent of classical French drama. Once again, it is structured more as a political thesis than a play, and Camus the thinker rarely allows Camus the playwright to let that pulse of all great theatre – **the Unexpected** – have free run. It is politically naive in its notion that revolutionary assassins should themselves die after their acts, a rather impractical idea at best. But it does address the question of political killing – and, not incidentally, in **Russia** – at a time when most Western intellectuals were turning a blind eye to the *gulags* and show trials in Eastern Europe, and asks once again whether the Just Society must be founded on the mass graves of its victims.

For all his sensitivity to post-war events, Camus was finding himself intellectually and politically **out of step** with his times. Outside of Soviet Communism, most of the European Left had found little political alternative to the recent Fascist onslaught. Even those who doubted, like Sartre, could find nothing better and had to admit that a good proportion of the working-class in Europe adhered to the Communist Party or was willing to follow its leadership.

Perhaps because he'd already been soured by CP manipulation in Algiers, or because his humanist tendencies prevented him from accepting **any** form of oppression, whether Fascist or Stalinist, Camus drew his line in the sand and refused the sort of compromises he saw being made all around him, especially in the Parisian intellectual *milieu.* The militancy of his *Résistance* phase now gave way to persistent calls for **moderation**.

Without going so far as to embrace the rampaging McCarthyism of the era, he began mounting a concerted attack against Marxism as a political philosophy and against Communism as a practical reality. He *nearly* added his name to those of **Arthur Koestler** (1905-83), **André Gide**, **Richard Wright** (1908-60), **Stephen Spender** (1909-95) etc., in the celebrated anti-Communist collection of memoirs and *mea culpas*, **The God That Failed** (1950).

Richard Wright

Arthur Koestler

André Gide

Stephen Spender

Louis Fischer

Six famous men tell how they changed their minds about Communism

The **GOD THAT FAILED**

Camus' "middle-of-the-road" position opened him up to the usual vitriolic barks from the CP kennel, calling him "*a fascist and bourgeois lackey*", who can be classed among "*the existentialists, liars, enemies of the people, enemies of mankind*".

"Existentialist", no less!

But much worse was yet to come, and from other writers whose opinions he had to take seriously.

Camus had already made his basic position clear in his seminal essay, "*Ni Victimes, Ni Bourreaux*" ("*Neither Victims Nor Executioners*", 1946). If the Absurd had to toy with the notion of suicide (individual experience), he was now talking about **Murder** (the collective). Calling our era "*the century of fear*", he paints a devastating picture of a world reduced to silence, abstraction and lack of human confidence, "*a world where murder is legitimized and human life considered futile*". Such terror can only have legitimacy if one believes that the end justifies the means, as do those philosophies, like Marxism, which turn historical necessity into an absolute.

As a remedy, Camus proposes "***a politically modest ideology, free of all messianism and rid of any nostalgia for paradise on earth***".

By the time he developed these ideas and those of the "*Remarque sur la révolte*" into the third part of his "revolt" cycle, *L'Homme Révolté* (*The Rebel*), Camus was one of the most famous men in France. There was no way that **anything** he said or wrote or did could now escape public scrutiny, and with this new book he opened up a Pandora's Box. There was, in each chapter, something for nearly everyone to despise and attack.

The trouble begins with the word "revolt" itself. Normally, we associate its usage with unrestrained freedom, with violence or aggression, at the very least a **clash** between rebellious forces and the *status quo*. Revolt goes beyond any law or morality or reason or religion which attempts to hold it down. Yet, as we have seen, by a curious twist of reasoning, Camus reins in the word to align it with **moderation**. It can be said that his interpretation of the word relies just as often on the passive notion of being "**revolted by**" something untenable, as the active "**revolting against**" it. Undoubtedly, he was playing with intellectual fire.

The crux of the matter, for Camus, is that the concentration camps and police states of the 20th century have been initially created in the name of revolution. Modern socialism, from its starting point as a rebellion against capitalism, is the crowning example, cynically using its own rebels as mere instruments towards a desired goal.

L'Homme Révolté is divided into five distinct sections, mixing figures from history, philosophy and literature into one enormous and often unwieldy rag-bag. Here we find again Nietzsche and Ivan Karamazov (from Dostoyevsky's novel), but equally the **Marquis de Sade** (1740-1814), the French poets **Arthur Rimbaud** (1854-91) and the **Comte de Lautréamont** (1846-70), **Karl Marx** (1818-83) and the pataphysical playwright **Alfred Jarry** (1873-1907), the mythological Greek titan Prometheus and the German philosopher **Friedrich Hegel** (1770-1831), but also Heathcliff from Emily Brontë's

Wuthering Heights, willing to kill for love, but never claiming this murder "*to be reasonable or justified by any system*". Each, in his own way, is "*un révolté*".

Yet the consequence of their rebellion is often violence and murder. The absence of God allowed the Jacobins to deify History and turn the French Revolution of 1789 into the Terror of 1793 in the name of **concepts** like Virtue and Liberty, using the guillotine as the high priest of their new cult. Camus even bemoans – how could he not? – the beheading of Louis XVI. "*It is a repulsive scandal to have presented the public assassination of a weak and good man as a great moment in our history.*"

In his demand for absolute freedom for himself and his sexual inclinations, the Marquis de Sade betrayed the idea of revolt in not respecting the freedom of others **not** to incline to his (de Sade's) desires. The final result of such unchecked liberty is totalitarianism.

Rebellious poets like Arthur Rimbaud turn into conformists. Revolutionary intellectuals glide sooner or later from wild anarchy to Communist discipline. Taking on the Surrealists, many of whom joined or were allied to the French Communist Party, Camus cites André Breton's famous maxim …

THE BASIC SURREALIST ACTION WOULD BE TO GO OUT INTO THE STREET, REVOLVER IN HAND, SHOOTING AT RANDOM INTO THE CROWD.

The only notable exceptions to the rule of betraying their original sense of revolt, according to Camus, are his "*meurtriers délicats*", the Russian Social Revolutionaries of 1905, with whom "***the spirit of revolt meets compassion for the last time in our history***".

Camus sets up and eliminates his targets one by one, but reserves the bulk of his ammunition for **Hegel**, with his insistence that only those values matter which will be justified in the long run by History. Man does not determine History, he is carried along by it. His freedom consists in his being absorbed in the necessary course of events.

Hegel also glorifies the State, claiming that the interest of each State is its own highest law. This, in itself, is extremely dangerous, for it can thus justify any form of State tyranny, a doctrine to which Camus would be naturally allergic.

For Camus, Marxism co-opts Hegel and turns itself into a religion, making a god of **History** which can accommodate all means to an End, even crime. In Hegelian thought, the victor is always right because his victory brings about the natural historical balance. If the Dictatorship of the Proletariat is a long-range and absolute goal, anchored in future necessity, then its relentless march cannot be deterred by anything, especially not human compassion. If State murder becomes a necessary weapon in achieving the final goal, then so be it.

In summary, man revolts against injustice anchored in the State. If his revolt is successful, it becomes revolution. But revolution leads inevitably to the creation of another State, and every State is unjust and oppressive. **What has begun in rebellion ends in tyranny**.

The question Camus asks is: how have men come to accept collective murder in the name of revolt and revolution? For him, revolution must never be an end in itself, but a means of achieving justice. For the non-Communist rebel, it is a matter of moving up from the absurd position of being without God, of liberating himself and **all other men**. "*Je me révolte donc nous sommes*", he declares, paraphrasing Descartes – "*I rebel therefore we are*".

Camus ends *L'Homme Révolté* by returning to one of his central themes: Mediterranean man. Opposing Greek or Mediterranean thinking to Germanic philosophy, he once again finds in the former the necessary "*mesure*" (moderation) to combat the latter. "*The great conflict of this century is … between German dreams and Mediterranean traditions … between the violence of eternal adolescence and virile strength … between history and nature.*" He tells us once again …

THE RUINS OF TIPASA

REVOLT IS IN ITSELF
MODERATION

… closing in the hope that Europe will leave its nihilism behind and embrace real rebellion, **measured** rebellion.

Some critics considered (and some still do) **L'Homme Révolté** to be a major contribution to modern political philosophy. And it must be said that some of its ideas do prefigure a way of thinking that would become *à la mode* some fifteen years later. Camus would surely have been more at home with the political movements of the 1960s. And that he would even dream of writing such a book against violence and nihilism in the face of the post-war intellectual cynicism which had set in, was in itself no mean achievement. But the harshness of his condemnations and absolute declarations – "*slavery is the only real passion in the twentieth century*" – rubbed most critics (not the public; it became a best-seller) the wrong way. Camus was asking for trouble.

He got it. For certain Marxist critics he would become "*the philosopher of myth and abstract freedom, the writer of illusion*". There was the Surrealist **André Breton** (1896-1966) who could not stomach the attacks on Rimbaud and Lautréamont, widely considered the forerunners of the French movement. Breton accused Camus of "*the worst kind of conservatism and conformity*". Moreover, responding – quite correctly – to the notion of "*mesure*" …

There would be many other attacks from both Left and Right, and Camus seemed to take each one personally, feeling the need to exercise his right to reply publicly to many of them. The most celebrated of these polemics began in 1952 with a review by the Marxist author Francis Jeanson in the magazine ...

Les Temps Modernes

7° année   **REVUE MENSUELLE**   n°79

Directeur : JEAN-PAUL SARTRE

Mai 1952

EXPOSÉS

FRANCIS JEANSON. — Albert Camus ou l'âme révoltée

... edited by none other than Jean-Paul Sartre. Jeanson argued in effect that Camus was struggling against history and direct political action. What's more, by dealing with the crimes of left-wing revolutionaries, Camus was inadvertently giving solace to the *bourgeoisie*.

Camus' reply was addressed to "*Monsieur le Directeur*" of *Les Temps Modernes*, a not-so-subtle barb at Sartre. Claiming that Jeanson had misread his book which was not a refusal of history, but of historical movements which use the end to justify the means, Camus then turned and went into counter-attack mode, citing "*those bourgeois intellectuals who try to deny their origins, even at the price of contradiction or of doing violence to their own intelligence*".

Monsieur le Directeur was livid, and replied in kind with nineteen pages of polemics mixed with personal remarks ...

My dear Camus, our friendship was never easy, but I'm going to miss it.

Where is Meursault, Camus? Where is Sisyphus? Where are those heartfelt Trotskyists preaching permanent revolution? No doubt assassinated or in exile.

There is in you a violent and ceremonious dictatorship, built upon an abstract bureaucracy which tries to make its morality the law of the land.

And, a final twist of the Existentialist knife ...

I don't believe you are the brother of the unemployed Communist from Bologna or the miserable day-labourer in Indochina ... struggling against the colonialists. Maybe you once were poor but you are not any longer; you are a bourgeois, like Jeanson and myself.

Sartre was not a Stalinist and did not turn a blind eye to the bitter realities of the Soviet Union. Neither was he a member of the French Communist Party, but he felt it was the only living alternative for the Left, considering its vast working-class membership. In this respect, he was much more in step with his era than Camus, who flirted in his disillusion now and again with a more human-faced social democracy as could be found then in Sweden or in Britain, but dreamed more of his "virile brotherhood" of *combattants* from the Mediterranean. His final word on this, one of the great intellectual polemics of its time, was, in referring to Sartre …

Camus' lingering importance as a non-fiction writer is probably less tied to a philosophical-historical-literary tome like **L'Homme Révolté** than to his crisp, hard-nosed essays and passionate committed journalism. With the passing of *Combat* into private hands in 1947, Camus found himself for a time without a means of direct mass communication at his disposal.

Nonetheless, his sense of engagement in the early 1950s was total, and this may be his true gift to intellectual activity in our time. The celebrated man of letters had become, with or without his pen, a full-time **advocate**. And this without allegiance to any party or organization. His actions now reflected his "declaration of faith", written in the last days of his stint with *Alger Républicain* in 1939 …

TODAY, WHEN ALL PARTIES HAVE BETRAYED, WHERE POLITICS HAS DEBASED EVERYTHING, THE ONLY THING LEFT FOR A MAN IS THE CONSCIOUSNESS OF HIS SOLITUDE AND HIS FAITH IN HUMAN AND INDIVIDUAL VALUES.

In his new **solitude** Camus would never show more **solidarity**, giving way to the French equation/pun ***solitaire-solidaire***, which he would later employ in one of his short stories. He was active in most of the major causes of his time.

A virulent opponent of Franco all his life, he resigned from UNESCO in 1952 when the organization admitted Spain to its ranks.
"It isn't [the playwrights] *Calderón or Lope de Vega the democratic nations have just admitted into their society of educators, but rather Joseph Goebbels."*

He spoke out against the violent state repression of the workers' uprising in East Berlin in 1953 …

WHEN A WORKER, SOMEWHERE IN THE WORLD, APPROACHES A TANK WITH HIS BARE FISTS AND CRIES OUT THAT HE'S NOT A SLAVE, WHAT ARE WE IF WE REMAIN INDIFFERENT ?

… as well as the Soviet crushing of the Hungarian revolt in 1956.
"What Spain was for us twenty years ago, Hungary will be today."

In July 1953, after police opened fire on a peaceful Moslem demonstration in Paris, killing and wounding many, he spoke of "… *the old conspiracy of silence and cruelty which uproots Algerian workers, puts them in miserable slums and leads them in desperation to the point of violence, occasionally killing them."*

With Communist causes he was more circumspect, knowing well the CP tradition of exploiting and misdirecting innocent advocacy. But he was true to himself in defending the American Rosenberg couple, sentenced to death in the electric chair for being Soviet spies. It is pertinent to wonder if he would have done so had the death penalty not been involved.

If Camus was at the forefront of nearly all the major events of his time, none would involve him more nor wound him more personally than the outbreak of rebellion and, ultimately, war in his native Algeria.

In early 1954, the Vietnamese General Giap had routed the French army at the legendary battle of Dien Bien Phu, leading to the independence of Indochina from French rule.

This event gave courage to other liberation efforts throughout the French territories and, on 1 November 1954, dozens of colonial installations, military barracks, police stations, etc. were attacked or bombed in Algeria, chiefly by the newly formed *Front de libération nationale* (FLN). The echoes of that night can still be heard in France nearly fifty years later.

Albert Camus' position in the events which were to follow has been criticized, damned, lamented and often misconstrued, but it is mostly consistent with the basic moral through-line of his life. It must first of all be understood that, at the time of the uprising, nearly a million French Algerians – *les pieds-noirs* – were settled in the country, some of them already fifth or sixth generation to the first immigrant wave of the mid-19th century, and for whom France may have been a cultural and linguistic reference, but **not their country**, **not their homeland**.

Camus' understanding of the situation was that of an enlightened *pied-noir*.

ALGERIA ISN'T FRANCE, IT ISN'T EVEN ALGERIA, IT IS THIS UNKNOWN LAND, WITH ITS INCOMPREHENSIBLE NATIVES, ITS ANNOYING SOLDIERS AND EXOTIC FRENCHMEN LOST FAR AWAY IN A FOG OF BLOOD.

Camus would insist that the majority of French Algerians were not *cliché* colonialists "*with riding crops, cigars in their mouths, driving Cadillacs*", but ordinary working-class people, most of whom could and did live in harmony with the Moslem population. There is probably as much wish-fulfilment as truth in this, and most of the *pieds-noirs* were either small farmers, civil servants, teachers, etc., while the Arabs and Berbers represented most of the non-skilled labour.

Camus never ceased to speak out against the Moslems' lack of civil rights or the psychological suffering and deracination they had endured. But this was no reason to uproot the French Algerians who were, in his eyes, also "indigenous". Behind his objective reasoning was the stark reality of his mother and other members of his family still living in Algiers.

He would even go so far as to say – extraordinary coming from his lips …

IF THE VIOLENCE CONTINUES, THE DUTY, EVEN OF A MAN LIKE ME, WOULD BE TO RETURN TO HIS COMMUNITY BECAUSE IT WOULD BE IMPOSSIBLE TO REMAIN NEUTRAL.

For the FLN, there was nothing less than total independence, an Algerian state based on Islamic principles. Soon this would become the clarion call of much of the French Left as well, including Sartre and Malraux. Camus would not hear of it, and he refused to fathom the notion of an independent Algeria even when this was the only option left.

"IT'S EASY TO BE ANTI-COLONIALIST IN THE BISTROS OF MARSEILLE OR PARIS."

Camus saw a different alternative, a kind of federation of the two communities, each having equal rights, granting a certain autonomy to the Moslem population and the power to govern itself within the federation. In his "Letter to an Algerian Militant" (1955), he claims the two groups are "*condemned to live together*": "*… we are not enemies and we can live together happily in this land which is ours.*" This obviously sincere position, which brought much contempt on Camus, was at best naive, inasmuch as a large majority of French Algerians were in favour of keeping the *status quo* and would not dream of sharing equal rights with Arabs or agreeing to a redistribution of wealth.

In February 1956, mass demonstrations of *pieds-noirs* forced the French government to give up its initiatives for reform and a bloody cycle of killing was now well installed in Algeria.

There were now some 400,000 French soldiers in the country, far outnumbering FLN militants. But the nationalist movement could count on the support of a large majority of Arabs, and resorted mostly to bombings and hit-and-run terrorist tactics. Torture, mass killing, evacuation of villages was the French response.

In 1955, Camus had begun to write for the new daily newspaper *l'Express*. His brief was, naturally, the Algerian situation, and within eight months he had written thirty-five articles, "*L'Algérie Déchirée*" (Algeria Torn Apart), later collected under the title **Actuelles: Chronique Algérienne**.

Here, once again, is the great Camus, lucid and passionate, concrete and damning. Those who considered him "equivocal" on Algeria had only to read these articles. For him, the real culprits are not the French Algerians:

WHO HAS CAPSIZED ALL PROJECTS OF REFORM FOR THIRTY YEARS, IF NOT A PARLIAMENT ELECTED BY THE FRENCH ? WHO HAS CLOSED ITS EARS TO THE CRIES OF ARAB MISERY... IF NOT THE GREAT MAJORITY OF THE FRENCH PRESS ? AND WHO, IF NOT FRANCE, WITH ITS DISGUSTING GOOD CONSCIENCE, HAS WAITED UNTIL ALGERIA BLEEDS TO FINALLY REALIZE THAT SHE EXISTS ?

It is in this series of articles that he first publicly puts forward an idea which could only have come from him: **The Civil Truce**. This was not a question of cessation of hostilities – by 1956, it was too late to imagine that. He simply demanded that both sides agree to **spare the civilian population**. Nothing could be more consistent with his notion of "revolt". If there absolutely must be killing, keep it to a bare minimum and spare the innocent victims. It was the explicit message of *Les Justes*. Fresh out of solutions, like almost everyone else involved, this became his very last attempt to influence the Algerian events fast spiralling out of control.

* "Long Live the F.L.N.!"

On 22 January 1956, Camus put his reputation – and his life – on the line, helping to organize a public meeting in Algiers. On his arrival, he already began to receive death threats.

Outside the meeting-hall, the two camps, one led by the ultra hard-line *Front Français de l'Algérie*, the other an anonymous mass of Moslems from the Casbah, were already in place for a face-off …

Inside, Camus spoke, protected by an armed guard of Arabs who, unbeknownst to him, were all members of the FLN as were, cynically, the organizers of the meeting. Knowing the project was doomed to fail, they nonetheless took part, hoping to reap the political benefits one way or the other.

Inevitably, no one would heed the call, and the spontaneous violence in Algeria would lead to all-out war. For many *pieds-noirs*, Camus would be seen as a traitor for not taking a pro-French stand. For the Moslem fighters, as for much of the French Left, he was simply naive or, as the Algerian writer **Albert Memmi** (b. 1920) called him, "*Le Colonisateur de bonne volonté*" (the well-meaning colonizer).

The failure of the civil truce campaign brought Camus' public efforts to a standstill, although he would continue in private to help Moslem rebels condemned by the French courts. His starting point was still the notion of **limiting the damage**, although there was one curious omission here. When overwhelming evidence of French torture practices in Algeria surfaced in 1957, he said nothing, perhaps fearing for the lives of his mother and family, should he appear to be taking sides.

In a last essay entitled "*Algérie 1958*", he attempted to support some kind of federation of different cultures on the Swiss model or even a vague form of "French commonwealth", **anything** short of independence. He was more and more convinced now – being a visionary, but also blinded by the reactionary tendencies of his era – that there was a Communist conspiracy afoot in his homeland, that Egypt was behind a "new Arab imperialism" supported by the Russians whose aim was to foment unrest and revolution in the Middle East and in African colonial territories "*in order to encircle Europe from the south*".

Still, he knew that virtually no one was listening to him any more.

THIS IS THE LAST WARNING — BEFORE GOING SILENT ONCE AGAIN — OF A WRITER WHO HAS SERVED THE CAUSE OF ALGERIA FOR TWENTY YEARS.

On the way to Silence, he would prepare some of his finest fiction – those stories dealing with Algeria in the collection, **L'Exil et le royaume** (**Exile and the Kingdom**, 1957), the crowning jewel amongst them being the critically-unsung masterpiece …

Daru, a French Algerian schoolteacher, has been posted high in the northern mountains. This is no longer the usual hot, dry desert landscape, but a bleak, snowy terrain above scattered Arab hamlets …

THE REGION WAS A CRUEL PLACE TO LIVE IN... BUT DARU HAD BEEN BORN THERE. EVERYWHERE ELSE HE FELT IN EXILE.

Daru's task is obviously to teach French history and culture, but the twenty or so local native children have stopped coming to school because of the weather.

Daru, "*living like a monk in the remote schoolhouse*", is taken by surprise by the arrival of the *gendarme* Balducci and an Arab prisoner.

This is the very beginning of the Algerian insurgency. Balducci explains that the authorities are expecting a revolt and that all *pieds-noirs*, Daru included, are called upon to "*mobilize*".

Still, Daru declares his intention not to hand the man over to the authorities. Balducci reminds him that he is ordered to do so, and gives him a revolver in case he needs to defend himself. Alone with his "guest", Daru is compelled to reflect on their situation.

NO ONE IN THIS DESERT, NEITHER HE NOR HIS GUEST, MATTERED MUCH. AND YET, DARU KNEW, NEITHER OF THEM COULD REALLY LIVE OUTSIDE OF THIS DESERT.

Daru feels compelled to act the "host". He cooks and, to the Arab's astonishment, shares his meal with him.

THE ARAB STARED AT HIM OPEN MOUTHED. OBVIOUSLY, HE DIDN'T UNDERSTAND.

During the night, Daru tries to sleep, but is agitated by the Arab's presence in the bed across the room. At play here – and subtly – is a metaphor for the entire Algerian situation as understood by Camus. The two men are compelled to share a room. Daru is non-violent, but he thinks of the revolver Balducci has given him when the Arab suddenly gets up in the middle of the night. Neither one trusts the other, but companionship is forced upon them. There are echoes of *La Peste* here …

HE'S ESCAPING. GOOD RIDDANCE !

MEN WHO SHARE THE SAME QUARTERS, SOLDIERS OR PRISONERS, DEVELOP A STRANGE BOND, AS IF, HAVING SHED THEIR DEFENCES ALONG WITH THEIR CLOTHING, THEY FIND THEMSELVES FACE TO FACE EACH EVENING, BEYOND THEIR DIFFERENCES, IN THE AGE-OLD COMMUNITY OF DREAMS AND FATIGUE.

In the morning they begin the enforced journey, but they come to a plateau where Daru suddenly halts, decides to go no further, and gives the Arab a package of provisions and some money.

THAT'S THE ROAD TO TINGUIT. IT'S A TWO-HOUR WALK TO THE ADMINISTRATION AND THE POLICE. THEY ARE WAITING FOR YOU.

OVER THERE IS THE PATH WHICH GOES ACROSS THE PLATEAU AFTER A DAY'S WALK YOU'LL FIND THE FIRST NOMADS. THEY'LL TAKE YOU IN AND GIVE YOU SHELTER, ACCORDING TO THEIR LAWS.

Leaving the "guest" to choose his own fate, Daru starts down the hill. At first the Arab is too panicked to move. Finally, looking back, Daru sees no one on the plateau. He remounts.

AND IN THE SLIGHT HAZE DARU, WITH A HEAVY HEART, COULD MAKE OUT THE ARAB MARCHING SLOWLY ON THE ROAD TO PRISON.

In the short time it has taken him to return to the classroom, a "revolutionary" message has been left behind on the blackboard, among the four French rivers: "*You handed our brother over. You'll pay for this.*"

DARU LOOKED AT THE SKY, THE PLATEAU AND, BEYOND IT, THE INVISIBLE LANDS STRETCHING OUT TO THE SEA.
IN THIS VAST COUNTRY WHICH HE HAD LOVED, HE WAS ALONE.

Who is the real "guest" here? The word "*hôte*" in French can mean both "host" and "guest". Is Daru the "host" in his own country or is he the real "guest" of the story? This question must surely have been in the subconscious of Albert Camus who, effectively, was living out Daru's dilemma in exile.

For once, the heavy hand of the **writer** was not covering the mouth and voice of the **storyteller**. In the twenty short pages of this magnificent story, all the human complexities of the Algerian situation are played out without commentary, and Camus was placing himself somehow outside the fray, lonelier than ever before.

In his last years, Camus took refuge again in the theatre – his first love – and it was even in his plans to run his own company. Curiously, his two most impressive dramatic works (*Requiem for a Nun*, 1956, and *The Possessed*, 1959) are technically not his own, but rather adaptations of great novels.

Here he had two master storytellers, **William Faulkner** (1897-1962) and Feodor Dostoyevsky, to create flesh and blood characters and a powerful dramatic line for him, while he, Camus, carved a shape which brought the social and political content out in stark relief.

Dostoyevsky's novel *The Possessed* had long since influenced him (its first sentence is echoed nearly word-for-word in that of *La Peste*). It was once again a means for him of dealing with revolutionary fanatics, and of restating his anti-terrorist arguments from *L'Homme Révolté*, in the thickening darkness of the Cold War.

Camus' real role here was as **director and interpreter**, not as a creative writer, and he became interested in all aspects of the craft – lighting, stage design – just as he had loved to work with lead type in the *Combat* print shop.

CATHERINE SELLERS AND ALBERT CAMUS DURING A REHEARSAL OF *REQUIEM FOR A NUN*.

Yet there was another, more personal, aspect of his return to the theatrical womb. Both of his main actresses, Maria Casarès and Catherine Sellers, were also his lovers, and no doubt seeing them (never together in the same play, of course!), and hearing them speak his words, night after night, directing them and correcting them, must have had a very private, erotic significance for Camus.

Despite his writer's cramp, Camus was able to complete one last novel in these final years, a long, self-conscious, humourless monologue which some critics, including Sartre, consider his best work of fiction …

Reflecting Camus' spirit, the sun has absconded and, instead of the hot landscapes of Algeria, there is nothing left but the desperate, stagnant gloom of Amsterdam.

The "judge-penitent", Jean-Baptiste Clamence, an ex-Parisian lawyer in Dutch exile, holds court before a silent listener in a series of confessions. No doubt there is much of Camus in this particular John the Baptist crying in the wilderness. All of his hurt is on display, including his dispute with Sartre. He attacks those "*professional humanists*" and "*the conviction of an intellectual predicting the classless society*". But the main object of his loathing is himself.

His relation to women is in many ways that of Camus.

And indeed it is a woman who forms the central pivot (and virtually the only real scene of **action**) in the book. One night, on the Pont-Royal in Paris, Clamence sees a young woman leaning over the parapet. A few seconds later he hears the sound of her jumping into the Seine. He fails to react, lets her drown, and is haunted by this for the rest of his life.

It is primarily this which forces him to give up his country and position, and seek the dark oblivion of Amsterdam.

There is, too, a nostalgia for Camus' lost Algeria, expressed indirectly through Clamence …

In his "*prière d'insérer*", an insert which French authors sometimes have slipped into their published books, Camus asked: "*Where does the confession begin, and where the accusation? Does the man who speaks in this book put himself on trial, or his entire era?*" And clearly this is what he wanted from the novel. But, in the end, the pointing finger merely turns back upon itself, condemns primarily Camus/Clamence, leaving him little more than his usual fascination with (in this case self-imposed) arrest and execution.

In 1957, Camus produced a book of immense importance, but which, curiously, is scarcely known to the public and only figures as a kind of addendum to critical commentaries on his work. This is his long essay *Réflexions sur la guillotine*, published together with Arthur Koestler's complementary work on hanging in Britain, under the collective title *Réflexions sur la peine capitale* (*Reflections on Capital Punishment*).

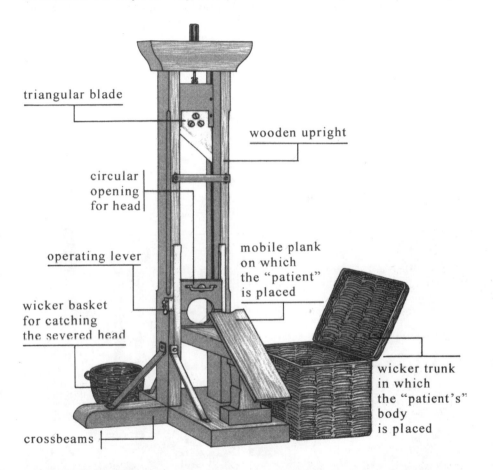

triangular blade

wooden upright

circular
opening
for head

operating lever

mobile plank
on which
the "patient"
is placed

wicker basket
for catching
the severed head

wicker trunk
in which
the "patient's"
body
is placed

crossbeams

It was inevitable that Camus would go back to the story of his father witnessing an execution, but his essay is not merely anecdotal. With hanging only recently abolished in Britain, and with the guillotine still in use in France and the electric chair in the US, Camus was adding his influential voice to a campaign whose ultimate goal was more than symbolic. War was raging in Algeria, the vast majority of French voters were in favour of the death penalty, and its elimination was an uphill battle.

There are no literary references here, no "philosophizing", and his prose has the concrete, muscular quality of his best journalism. Dismantling the traditional argument that capital punishment has an "exemplary" function, Camus points out the contradiction that all "public" executions are in fact **hidden** from the public. He makes the suggestion, only half ironically, "*to place the guillotine on a scaffold, on the Place de la Concorde* [in Paris], *at two o'clock in the afternoon, invite the public and televise the ceremony for those who can't make it.*"

To make his particular point about the guillotine – the historical essence of **French State sadism** – Camus resorts to all the ghoulish details, in hopes of "*showing the obscenity hidden behind a cloak of words*".

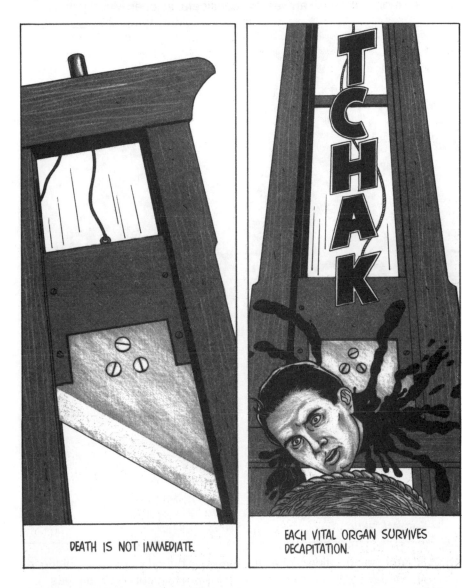

DEATH IS NOT IMMEDIATE.

EACH VITAL ORGAN SURVIVES DECAPITATION.

He cites numerous medical experts, pointing out that the guillotined body undergoes a crisis of *delirium tremens* and continues to agitate for twenty minutes after beheading.

Camus argues that capital punishment destroys the humanity of a prisoner insofar as he has to live with the inevitability of his penalty on a permanent basis, sometimes for months or even years before, one day, without warning, it simply arrives. He considers, as does Meursault …

EVERYTHING HAPPENS OUTSIDE HIS CONTROL. HE'S NO LONGER A HUMAN BEING …

… BUT RATHER A THING WAITING TO BE MANIPULATED BY THE EXECUTIONER.

Camus' strongest position – one which can be hurled in the faces of those who even today continue to support capital punishment – is that it has **nothing whatever** to do with deterrence of violent crime.

*"Let's call it by its real name … and recognize it for what it is: **vengeance**."*

But he goes further, following the logic of **L'Homme Révolté**.

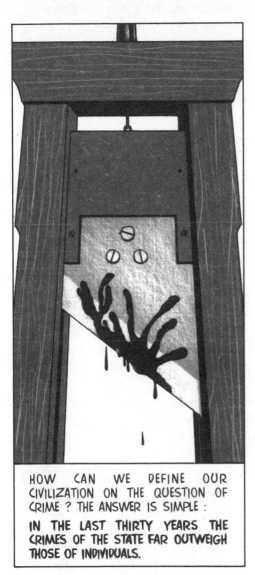

HOW CAN WE DEFINE OUR CIVILIZATION ON THE QUESTION OF CRIME ? THE ANSWER IS SIMPLE :

IN THE LAST THIRTY YEARS THE CRIMES OF THE STATE FAR OUTWEIGH THOSE OF INDIVIDUALS.

And, in this context, capital punishment becomes **premeditated murder** by the State, one which "*tarnishes our society*". Camus now reminds his readers, in no uncertain terms, "***that the life of a human being is above the State***", a sentiment which would easily have won him acclaim from radical movements ten years later, but which surely must have sounded subversive in the 1950s.

At the end of **Réflexions sur la guillotine**, Camus expresses the hope that in the "*united Europe of tomorrow*", the abolition of the death penalty would be "*Article 1 of the European Code*". The French State would not heed his words until 1901, 24 years later. But it was clear that, through his persistent humanitarian advocacy, he had become the primary author of the modern European "conscience", and this was the chief basis on which he was awarded the Nobel Prize for Literature in 1957.

By European standards, and by those of the Swedish Academy, the prize was – as it nearly always is – politically correct. In France, the award tended to gain Camus more enemies and isolate him even further. He was the second youngest author ever to receive the prize, and this led his detractors to conclude that it meant his work was effectively over.

In Sweden, in the heat of numerous Nobel conferences and speeches and debates, there occurred a scene which has become a legendary part of his biography.

During a meeting at Stockholm University, Camus was verbally attacked by an Arab student who claimed the author only militated for Eastern Europe but not for Algeria. For years, Camus had been haunted by the spectre of his family caught in the Algerian crossfire. Now he fired back …

I HAVE TO DENOUNCE BLIND TERRORISM IN THE STREETS OF ALGIERS, WHICH MIGHT ONE DAY STRIKE MY MOTHER OR MY FAMILY.

I BELIEVE IN JUSTICE, BUT I'LL DEFEND MY MOTHER BEFORE JUSTICE.

This remark sent shockwaves through the Lefter-than-thou French intellectual circles. It was claimed that Camus was abandoning "justice", which had been his personal keyword for decades, that private concerns were more vital to him than the Algerian cause, etc.

Ironically, by this time, Camus' discreet behind-the-scenes activities had saved numerous Algerian militants from the guillotine, and that was the gist, not only of his Algerian position, but of his lifelong struggle against **Absurd Death**. His mother was only one of the innocents he had hoped to save with his notion of a civil truce, but, above all, she was **his mother**! The creator of the famous literary character condemned to death for, in effect, not loving his mother enough, was saying clearly that a single human life comes first before a political cause, that there has been enough killing and enough Absurd Death, and finally, the man so often criticized for his coldness and distance was stating a human preference, not just standing up abstractly for "humanity", but acting like a **mother-loving son**.

His own Absurd Death was not far off. In these last years he bought a house and spent a large part of his time in the Provençal village of Lourmarin, close enough to the Mediterranean to bring him a whiff and a wink of North Africa.

In May 1958, a *coup* led by right-wing military officers and conservative *pieds-noirs*, convinced that France was giving up Algeria, had the indirect result of bringing Charles de Gaulle back to power in Paris and bringing the Fourth French Republic to an end. But soon de Gaulle was promising "self-determination" for Algerians. Camus was planning to campaign against independence if the question were put to a referendum. At the same time, he supported a movement to help conscientious objectors who sought alternative service rather than going to fight in Algeria.

Meanwhile, he was waiting for word from Paris to see if he would be given his own theatre company. He was trying to write his new novel and planning for a third series, including a play and a book of essays, this time on the theme of Love, although he complained to friends that the writing-spring had run dry. From afar, he was trying to organize his ever more complex *vie sentimentale*, sending off *rendezvous* messages to his three current lovers, all waiting for him to return to Paris.

In the first days of January 1960, after having bought himself a train ticket, it was suggested he drive back to Paris with his friend and publisher Michel Gallimard and his family. Camus, clearly out of touch with the French "*esprit*", detested fast driving. Years before, he had said that to die in an automobile accident would be "*une mort imbécile*".

AFTERWORD

Nearly forty years after his death, Albert Camus has suffered the worst fate of all for a committed writer: he has become a classic. In its French editions alone, *L'Étranger* (which remains his foremost masterpiece) has sold over 6 million copies, one of the top-selling books in the history of French publishing. It has been translated into more than forty languages and had the honour of being banned in Maoist China for "appealing to *bourgeois* taste" with its emphasis on solitude.

Several generations of French high school students have been forced to think of Camus with repugnance as a highly probable subject on their *baccalauréat* exams. One of the chief manuals for *lycée* students on Camus' "philosophy" claims he never threatened "*anything in our Christian or capitalist civilization*".

Camus' real heyday came only one short generational leap after his own disappearance. He would become a hero of the New Left in the 1960s, chiefly for his elucidation of the Absurd as found in *Le Mythe de Sisyphe.* The expression "theatre of the absurd", coined by the critic Martin Esslin, is taken chiefly from Camus, and has come to signify, rightly or wrongly, the plays of **Samuel Beckett** (1906-89), **Eugene Ionesco** (1912-94), **Jean Genet** (1910-86) and others whose world seems bereft of direction or purpose.

Yet, even more vital to his image in the 1960s (and today one of his lasting contributions) was his insistence, in his last years, on the **priority of the Citizen over State Power**. He envisaged a society "*free of the myth of sovereignty, a revolutionary force not backed up by police, and human freedom which is not subservient to money*". In this he was following a radical French tradition which had tended to get lost in the intellectual investment which so many had made in Soviet Russia in the 1930s and 40s.

In his argument that the State has no moral right to take the life of a citizen, he is still far ahead of his time, not only with regard to official murder in the Third World but to the capital-punishing United States as well.

In attacking the deification of History, he was being true to himself and to the Absurd. For why dispense with God only to worship a Concept, only to be manipulated by commissars instead of priests? The Marxist Left never forgave him for arguing that the human spirit was stronger than History.

> HISTORY HAS NO EYES, AND ITS JUSTICE SHOULD BE REPLACED BY THE JUSTICE CONCEIVED IN THE SPIRIT.

Camus' stance on Soviet Russia and on the bankruptcy of the Communist movement seems, in retrospect, prophetic. He was one of a few prominent Western intellectuals to question the Marxist heritage long before it became fashionable to do so. He was saying in 1945 what other believers would only come to proclaim in disenchantment after the overwhelming evidence of riots in East Berlin in 1953, the Hungarian uprising in 1956 and (the last holdouts) the Soviet invasion of Czechoslovakia in 1968.

At the same time, he was not immune to (although vaccinated against) one of the great **plagues** of the second half of the 20th century: a rampant, flea- and rat-infested anti-Communist hysteria which also has the blood of many innocents on its hands.

With regard to Algeria, he was certainly blinded by personal considerations and definitely against the grain of modern history in opposing independence at a time when such movements were aflame all across Africa.

Yet he was able to see the terrible dilemma of those French Algerians anchored in North African soil for generations, those whom other French intellectuals (and eventually the French government) were willing to sacrifice.

With independence, some 800,000 *pieds-noirs* were uprooted from the only homeland they had known, most of them emigrating to metropolitan France which accepted them only half-heartedly. That the kind of realistic coexistence between opposing communities which he foresaw has been shown to work (however grudgingly) in unlikely places like post-independence Zimbabwe and even South Africa attests to the power of Camus' vision (as well as his short-sightedness regarding independence) and puts into wider perspective his immediate political goals.

There is one aspect of his Algerian fears which joins his anti-totalitarian commentary in **L'Homme Révolté**, citing the inevitable corruption of revolutionary movements. For the group of liberation fighters claiming an independent Algeria eventually evolved into an encrusted, militaristic group of men bent on retaining – and not knowing how to share – power, men who bear at least some of the responsibility for what can only be called the "holocaust" taking place in that country today.

Camus' final response to the Algerian question might have become his most profound. The recent publication of his great unfinished novel **Le Premier Homme** (**The First Man**) is one of the chief reasons for what might be called a "Camus renaissance" in the 1990s. In the handwritten drafts of this powerful work, you can see the Writer and the Storyteller wrestling for domination, and the result (if it can be called that in its wild state) is a new beginning for Camus. Never had he written so **personally** in his fiction, and never had he given such long breath to the infinite subtle details of literature. He was experiencing that magic moment (the Control Commission in his brain had rarely allowed it to happen before) when a work of fiction **writes itself**.

Portions of the novel take place during the uprising against the colonial settlers. Jacques Cormery (Albert Camus) returns to Algeria for the last time in search of his country, his roots, the father he has never known. Some local prefects have already given the French Algerian settlers the order to evacuate their land. Cormery hears the story of one farmer who emptied his wine vats, flooded his fields with brackish water and hooked up a plough to his tractor …

FOR THREE DAYS, WITHOUT SAYING A WORD, HE UPROOTED HIS VINES OVER THE WHOLE EXTENT OF HIS LAND, LOOKING NEITHER AT THE MOUNTAINS ON THE HORIZON, NOR AT THE ARABS WHO'D COME TO WATCH HIM DO IT, THEY TOO SAYING NOTHING.

Cormery then meets a farmer who refuses to leave.

I'VE SENT MY FAMILY ON TO ALGIERS BUT I'M GOING TO DIE HERE. THEY CAN'T UNDERSTAND THAT IN PARIS. ASIDE FROM US, YOU KNOW WHO UNDERSTANDS THAT?

THE ARABS.

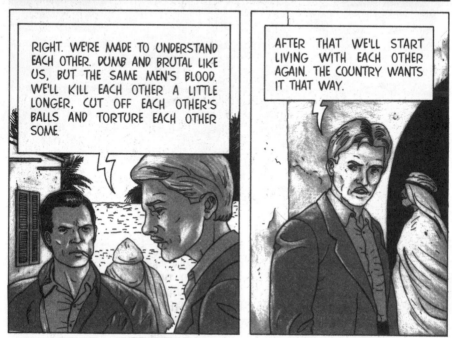

RIGHT. WE'RE MADE TO UNDERSTAND EACH OTHER. DUMB AND BRUTAL LIKE US, BUT THE SAME MEN'S BLOOD. WE'LL KILL EACH OTHER A LITTLE LONGER, CUT OFF EACH OTHER'S BALLS AND TORTURE EACH OTHER SOME.

AFTER THAT WE'LL START LIVING WITH EACH OTHER AGAIN. THE COUNTRY WANTS IT THAT WAY.

Later, Cormery and several other settlers walk through the local village, showing the two communities in co-habitation, yet already interlocked in the unspoken tragedy of approaching war.

TODAY WAS SUNDAY, BUT THE ARMY'S PSYCHOLOGICAL WARFARE SERVICE HAD INSTALLED LOUDSPEAKERS ON THE BANDSTAND. THE CROWD WAS CHIEFLY ARAB, BUT THEY WERE NOT STROLLING AROUND THE SQUARE. THEY STOOD STILL AND LISTENED TO THE ARABIC MUSIC PLAYING BETWEEN SPEECHES, AND THE FRENCHMEN LOST IN THE CROWD ALL HAD THE SAME SOMBRE LOOK, TURNED TOWARDS THE FUTURE, AS THOSE WHO HAD COME HERE LONG AGO ON THE *LABRADOR* ... THE SAME SUFFERING, FLEEING FROM MISERY AND PERSECUTION, FINDING ONLY SORROW AND STONE.

In one of the novel's climactic scenes, Cormery leaves his native Solferino and flies to Algiers.

THE MEDITERRANEAN SEPARATES TWO WORLDS IN ME, ONE WHERE MEMORIES AND NAMES ARE PRESERVED IN MEASURED SPACES, THE OTHER WHERE WIND AND SAND WIPE OUT ALL TRACES OF MEN ON THE GREAT OPEN SPACES.

Then, he thinks one last time of his father, the **first man** both for him and for the "new world" of Algeria …

"He accepted now with a sort of strange joy that death would bring him back to his true country and … cover up that strange and ordinary man who had grown up, built in poverty … on a happy shore and in the light of the first mornings of the world, in order to confront, alone, with neither memory nor faith, the world of the men of his times and its frightful and exhilarating history."

He was talking about his father and talking about himself. He was summing up and punctuating as never before, letting his endless sentences wander into un-Camusian subordinate clauses, then into interminable paragraphs, without carving them into crisp journalistic statements. A few more months perhaps, and it would have been finished.

Reading Camus in English

Camus' fiction, like that of many other writers of his time, was the victim of the curious attempt to "anglicize" his language and concerns in the 1950s and 60s. Thus *The Stranger*, not only falsely rendered as "The Outsider", was translated in a plodding, stilted way. Now the book has been re-translated by Matthew Ward, with strict fidelity to Camus' style, as is the case with David Hapgood's rendering of *The First Man*.

With one or two exceptions, the plays fall into the trap of mimicking Camus' rhetorical style, which can often work in French but rarely when rendered into English. With the notable exception of *The Possessed*, the English versions are thoroughly un-actable, giving the impression that this is true of the originals, which is not the case. It can only be hoped that, as part of the current Camus revival, new translations will be the order of the day.

Camus' numerous books of essays and notebooks are generally well translated and have been dispersed among three English volumes: *The Myth of Sisyphus and Other Essays* (1955); *Resistance, Rebellion and Death* (1961); and *Selected Essays and Notebooks* (1970).

The newly translated biography of Camus by Olivier Todd (*Camus*, 1997) is full of journalistic tidbits and has had access to recently released information. It sheds new light especially on the author's love life. But the standard biography remains that of Herbert R. Lottman (*Albert Camus*), written in English in 1979. Where Todd's work is a huge effort at fact-gathering and day-by-day accounts, Lottman's is far more profound and insightful. Probably the best book in English about Camus' work is Philip Thody's *Albert Camus 1913–1960*. An excellent work on the plays is E. Freeman, *The Theatre of Albert Camus: A Critical Study*.

Author's Note

All translations from the French are my own. Occasionally it has been necessary to truncate fictional dialogue in order to fit the concision of comic book speech. This is completely intentional. DZM

David Zane Mairowitz is the author of *Kafka for Beginners* (with Robert Crumb), as well as *Wilhelm Reich for Beginners* and *The Radical Soap Opera*. His plays for radio are produced in over twenty countries, and his radiophonic opera, *The Voluptuous Tango*, won the Prix Italia Special Prize and the Sony Prize in 1997.

Alain Korkos is a cartoonist for several French magazines. He also illustrates newspaper articles and designs book jackets and childrens' books. His first novel, *En Attendant Eliane*, has been awarded prizes in France and Canada.

Index